Native American Entrepreneurs

Native American Entrepreneurs

Ron Sheffield
J. Mark Munoz

BEP BUSINESS EXPERT PRESS

Native American Entrepreneurs
Copyright © Business Expert Press, LLC, 2020.

First published in 2020 by
Business Expert Press, LLC
222 East 46th Street, New York, NY 10017
www.businessexpertpress.com

ISBN-13: 978-1-94897-641-1 (paperback)
ISBN-13: 978-1-94897-642-8 (e-book)

Business Expert Press Entrepreneurship and Small Business Management Collection

Collection ISSN: 1946-5653 (print)
Collection ISSN: 1946-5661 (electronic)

Cover and interior design by S4Carlisle Publishing Services Private Ltd., Chennai, India
Cover image licensed by Ingram Image, StockPhotoSecrets.com

First edition: 2020

10 9 8 7 6 5 4 3 2 1

Printed in the United States of America.

Abstract

Native American entrepreneurs are important contributors to the American economy and social landscape. Faced with numerous challenges, many Native American entrepreneurs have learned to transcend tough obstacles, leverage resources, and strategically pursue opportunities to achieve business success. This book captures the entrepreneurial stories and mindsets of contemporary Native Americans.

Keywords

entrepreneurship; entrepreneurs; indigenous entrepreneurship; indigenous survival; Native American; Native American entrepreneurs; ethnic entrepreneur; minority entrepreneur; entrepreneurial mindset; entrepreneurial success; entrepreneurial stories; contemporary entrepreneurship; entrepreneurship theories; American entrepreneurship

Contents

Acknowledgments

This book has been developed as part of a formal research study of Native American entrepreneurs. Approved through the Institutional Review Board (IRB #018.059) at Christopher Newport University (CNU) in Newport News, Virginia, 20 structured interviews with indigenous tribal members were compiled.

Dr. Ron Sheffield, member of the Quechan Indian Tribe of Fort Yuma, Arizona, would like to thank and acknowledge a select team of research assistants at CNU. These dedicated students assisted with this critical research during the fall of 2018 and spring of 2019: Katelyn Ries, Emma Seguin, James Edwards, Mary "Catie" Adams, David Buchanan, Jacqueline Kotoriy, Nicole Oliashirazi, Natalie Schauer, Celina Eosso, and Alexis Helmer.

Each of these brilliant students was chosen to assist with this rare research because of their natural ability to see the world as a place of opportunity, greatness, and never-ending compassion. When asked about family history and entrepreneurship, one respondent's words synthesized the Native American perspective beautifully:

> I guess you can say my mother. My mom always had this Hustler vibe about her to make sure all of her children were fed and had a roof over our head. Yes, because I saw how hard my mother would work to keep lights on. I told myself, one day I would want to take care of my mother so she would never have to work that hard ever again.

CHAPTER 1

Introduction

Everyone who is successful must have dreamed of something.

—Maricopa

Indigenous people of North America (often referred to as "Native Americans") share a common past that includes colonization (Walters and Takamura 2015) and an ongoing, largely internalized, position of conflict with the U.S. federal government. While a merging of cultures may have produced a modern, economically powerful America, extensive complexities remain between indigenous people and the very recent visitors to this prosperous land, the U.S. federal government.

In recent years, the global community has seen major breakthroughs in the fields of management and entrepreneurship, as well as in technology. While countless research efforts have centered on corporate, as well as mainstream business agenda, few studies have focused on minority and ethnic groups.

Arguably, few cultures are more historically relevant to North America than its indigenous people. Interestingly, as key contributors to the U.S. economy, there has been limited research on Native American entrepreneurship (Stewart and Schwartz 2007). However, only very recently have researchers worked to define this unique section of entrepreneurs. Hindle and Lansdowne (2005) define indigenous entrepreneurship as, "the creation, management and development of new ventures by Indigenous people for the benefit of Indigenous people" (p. 132).

Hindle and Moroz (2010) attempt to formalize the field of indigenous entrepreneurship as an independent body of academic research, and the researcher posited that there are two significant issues that form the basis for research findings. These challenges include defining the "role of 'community' as a consideration affecting all forms and processes of Indigenous entrepreneurship" and considering "the multi-faceted importance of 'land' (where the word 'land' embraces all issues ranging from physical terrain to formal property rights)" (p. 372). As recently as 2017, Colbourne posits, "Native American entrepreneurship is not just about money, it is about history, tradition, culture and language embedded in time and traditional territory" (p. 59).

Despite the lack of attention, the Native American culture and economic position has undergone substantial changes. For instance, as a result of economic development initiatives, Native Americans have witnessed improvement in both wealth and income (Agustin 2013).

Table 1.1 offers an overview of American Indian and Native Alaskans in the United States.

Information from Table 1.1 suggests that (1) the number of American Indian and Native Alaskans in the United States is significant enough to make an economic contribution, (2) they are geographically dispersed and diverse, and (3) many are fairly young and can make strong economic contribution in the future.

Native Americans have made a mark in several industries. Some of the economic activities Native Americans have been involved in include utilization of natural resources and food systems, energy, and international trading (National Congress of American Indians 2013).

The depth and scope of their economic contribution has been significant. For instance, according to Schapp (2010), a number of tribes have created successful gaming enterprises whose revenues and jobs are bringing about major social benefits, reducing welfare transfers, improving the quality of service programs (i.e., emergency services), increasing health outcomes (i.e., nursing homes), and increasing educational attainment (p. 375). Yet, despite evident successes, countless challenges and barriers exist. Some of these include:

High rate of poverty—President Barack Obama noted the fact that as a result of discrimination, Native Americans face limited opportunities leading to unemployment and high incidence of poverty (White House Office of the Press Secretary 2013). With low employment and economically challenged communities, they are among the most economically disadvantaged in the United States (Agustin 2013).

Table 1.1 Overview on American Indian and Native Alaskans in the United States

Minority	In the United States, there are approximately 6.6 million American Indians and Alaska Natives, and they comprise about 2% of the total population.
Larger number in 21 states	There are 21 states with over 100,000 or more American Indian and Alaska Native residents, these are: California, Oklahoma, Texas, Arizona, New York, New Mexico, Washington, North Carolina, Florida, Michigan, Colorado, Alaska, Illinois, Oregon, Minnesota, Georgia, Pennsylvania, Virginia, Ohio, Wisconsin, and New Jersey. The States with the highest concentration of American Indian and Alaska natives are: Alaska (19.5%), Oklahoma (13.6%), New Mexico (11.8%), South Dakota (10.3%), and Montana (8.3%).
Fairly young population	The median age of American Indian and Native Alaskans is 30.2 years, significantly younger than the U.S. median of 37.8 years.
Highly diverse	There are 326 federally recognized American Indian Reservations and 567 federally recognized Indian tribes in 2016.
Educated	With regard to education, 82.7% of American Indians and Native Alaskans had a high school diploma or GED certificate, 19.1% had a bachelor's degree or higher.
Multilingual	Approximately 27.1% of American Indians and Native Americans five years old or older spoke English, compared to 21.5% of the U.S. population.
Experience of income disparity and poverty	The median household income of American Indians and Native Alaskans is $38,500 compared to $55,775 for the nation. The incidence of poverty among American Indians and Native Alaskans is around 26.6%, the highest rate of any age group.
Relatively few homeowners	About 53.1% of American Indians and Native Alaskans own their own home compared to 63% of the overall population.
Economic contributors	American Indians and Native Alaskans are active in the workforce with involvement in management, business, science and art (26.4%), service (23.9%), and sales and office occupation (23.4%).
Business creators	American Indians and Native Alaskans own approximately 26,757 firms in the United States in 2014.

Source: Census.gov (2016).

Low entrepreneurial engagement—there is limited self-employment among the Native American community (Fairlie 2004). History has played a role in the diminished interest of Native Americans in capitalism and a preference for socialism (Miller 2001) since many tribes in the past years met their needs through subsidized welfare programs.

Educational challenges—Native Americans tend to perceive themselves as having less business education (Garsombke and Garsombke 2000).

Inadequate mentorship—lack of role models, along with social and cultural factors, pose barriers to Native American entrepreneurship (Stewart and Schwartz 2007).

Financial resource limitations—Native American entrepreneurs believe that lack of access to financial resources has impeded their venture's success (Dewees 2004).

Geographical issues—Native American entrepreneurs are challenged by isolated geographic location and lack of resources (Kauffman. org 2015).

Sociocultural factors—Native American entrepreneurs have been found to have a self-perception that is less objective and collectivist-leaning as compared to entrepreneurs of other races (Garsombke and Garsombke 2000).

Many Native Americans have overcome these barriers and made a significant impact in society. Successful American Indian–run companies are in diverse sectors, including human resources, construction, and government services (Indian Country Media Network 2011).

Examples of successful Native American entrepreneurs are shown in Table 1.2. This is not an exhaustive list but just a small snapshot of those that have made in-roads in entrepreneurship.

Studies have shown that Native American entrepreneurial spirit can be nurtured by supporting factors.

Education and infrastructure—Native Americans need support in the areas of health education and infrastructure in order to deal with the countless challenges they face (Agustin 2013).

Technical assistance—research suggests that technical assistance contributes to the success of Native American firms (Jorgensen and Taylor 2000).

Table 1.2 Examples of successful Native American entrepreneurs

Name	Position	Company	Industry	Headquarters
Ken Novotny	CEO and President	Consulting Services, Inc. (CSI)	Government services	Oklahoma
Jim Williamson	CEO	New West Technologies	Government services	Colorado
Paul Lombardi	CEO and President	TeraThink	IT services and management consulting	Virginia
Louie Wise III	President	Climate Control Mechanical Services	Construction company	Florida
Royce Cornelison	CEO and President	P&C Construction	General contracting	Oregon
Jeff Styers	President	Arrow Strategies	Staffing agency	Michigan
Kyle von Bucholz,	CEO	Federated Information Technologies	Professional services	Washington, DC
Vickie Wessel	President	Spirit Electronics	Electronics	Arizona
Bryan Billingsley	President	HEBCO	Engineering and technical services	Oklahoma
Stephen Mills	CEO and President	AQIWO	Information services	Virginia

Source: Indian Country Media Network (2011).

Entrepreneurial training—business training and technical support are among the most critical, yet underdeveloped development programs for Native American communities (Malkin et al. 2004).

Community support and mentorship—Native American entrepreneurs will succeed with independent management for entrepreneurial ventures, consistent regulation, educated financial players, and showcasing of successful stories of successful stories of Native American entrepreneurs (Kauffman.org 2015).

Cultivating entrepreneurship among Native Americans will not only change lives but will also ensure their future economic development. Entrepreneurship among Native American communities is a pathway for addressing challenges relating to poverty and lack of economic independence (Cornell and Kalt 2003).

The authors decided to pursue this pioneering research effort to advance the study of entrepreneurship and inspire Native Americans to engage in entrepreneurship.

This book is a study of Native American entrepreneurship and offers business insights from interviews with Native American entrepreneurs across America. The book comprises five chapters: Chapter 1, Introduction; Chapter 2, Research Methodology; Chapter 3, Native American Interviews; Chapter 4 features the Research Findings; and Chapter 5 is the Conclusion.

In order to understand some of the complexities surrounding this unique research, when asked how native people might respond to being asked sensitive questions about survival, growth, and identity, an appreciation for the indigenous perspective on entrepreneurship by one author's full-blood Quechan mother posited: "Be careful what you ask and be prepared to hear nothing" (Sheffield 2013, v).

This book is dedicated to all indigenous people across America. The authors hope the stories and the shared insights inspire not only indigenous youth and business enthusiasts but all entrepreneurs from around the world.

References

Agustin, A. 2013. "Native Americans and Jobs," *Policy Institute*. https://www. epi.org/publication/bp370-native-americans-jobs/, (accessed April 21, 2018).

Census.gov. 2016. "Facts for features: American Indian and Alaska Native heritage month: November 2016." https://www.census.gov/newsroom/facts-for-features/2016/cb16-ff22.html, (accessed April 20, 2018).

Colbourne, R. 2017. "An understanding of Native American Entrepreneurship." *Small Enterprise Research* 24, no. 1, pp. 49–61. doi:10.108 0/13215906.2017.1289856

Cornell, S., and J.P. Kalt. 2003. *Reloading the Dice: Improving the Chances for Economic Development on American Indian Reservations (2003–2002).* The Harvard Project on American Indian Economic Development.

Dewees, S. 2004. *Investing in Community: Community Development Financial Institutions in Native Communities.* Kyle, SD: First Nations Oweesta Corporation.

Fairlie, R.W. 2004. "Recent Trends in Ethnic and racial Business Ownership." *Small Business Economics* 23, pp. 203–218.

Walters, F., and J. Takamura. 2015. "The Decolonized Quadruple Bottom Line: A Framework for Developing Indigenous Innovation." *Wicazo Sa Review* 30, no. 2, pp. 77–99. doi:10.5749/wicazosareview.30.2.0077

Garsombke, D.J., and T.W. Garsombke. 2000. "Non-traditional vs. Traditional Entrepreneurs: Emergence of a Native American Comparative profile of Characteristics and Barriers." *Academy of Entrepreneurship Journal* 6, no. 1, pp. 93–100.

Hindle, K., and M. Lansdowne. 2005. "Brave Spirits on New Paths: Toward a Globally Relevant Paradigm of Indigenous Entrepreneurship Research." *Journal of Small Business and Entrepreneurship* 18, no. 2, pp. 131–141. https://0-search-proquest-com.read.cnu.edu/docview/214500585?accountid=10100, (accessed May 19, 2019).

Hindle, K., and P. Moroz. 2010. "Indigenous Entrepreneurship as a Research Field: Developing a Definitional Framework from the Emerging Canon." *International Entrepreneurship and Management Journal* 6, no. 4, pp. 357–385. doi: 10.1007/s11365-009-0111-x

Indian Country Media Network. 2011. "Inc ranks Top 10 American Indian Entrepreneurs." https://indiancountrymedianetwork.com/news/inc-ranks-top-10-american-indian-entrepreneurs/, (accessed April 20, 2018).

Jorgensen, M., and J.B. Taylor. 2000. "What Determines Indian Economic Success? Evidence from Tribal and Individual Indian Enterprises." *Red Ink* 8, no. 2, pp. 45–51.

Kauffman.org. 2015. "4 Ways to Spur Native American Entrepreneurship." https://www.kauffman.org/blogs/currents/2015/08/4-ways-to-spur-native-american-entrepreneurship, (accessed April 21, 2018.)

Malkin, J., B. Dabson, K. Pate, and A. Mathews. 2004. *Native Entrepreneurship: Challenges and Opportunities for Rural Communities*, CFED. https://community-wealth.org/sites/clone.community-wealth.org/files/downloads/report-malkin-et-al.pdf

Miller, R.J. 2001. Economic Development in Indian Country: Will Capitalism or Socialism Succeed? *Oregon Law Review* 80, pp. 757–859.

National Congress of American Indians. 2013. "Securing Our Futures." http://www.ncai.org/Securing_Our_Futures_Final.pdf, (accessed April 21, 2018).

Schaap, J.I. 2010. The Growth of the native American Gaming Industry: What Has the Past Provided, and What Does the future Hold? *American Indian Quarterly* 34, no. 3, pp. 365–389,407. https://0-search-proquest-com.read.cnu.edu/docview/734396670?accountid=10100, (accessed May 19, 2019).

Sheffield, R. 2013. "The Influence of Language on Culture and Identity: Resurgence of the Quechan Native American Tribal Language (Order No. 3557504)." Available from ProQuest Central; ProQuest Dissertations & Theses Global. (1346231646). https://0-search-proquest-com.read.cnu.edu/docview/1346231646?accountid=10100, (accessed May 19, 2019).

Stewart, D., and R. G. Schwartz. 2007. "Native American Business Strategy: A Survey of Northwest US Firms." *International Journal of Business Performance Management* 9, no. 3, pp. 259–277.

White House Office of the Press Secretary. December 4, 2013. "Remarks by the President on Economic Mobility." http://www.whitehouse.gov/the-press-office/2013/12/04/remarks-president-economic-mobility, (accessed April 21, 2018).

CHAPTER 2

Research Methodology

Tell me and I'll forget. Show me, and I may not remember. Involve me, and I'll understand.

—Tribe Unknown

There were at least five reasons that motivated the authors to conduct this study:

1. Capture a mindset—how do Native American entrepreneurs think? How do they navigate challenges and uncover opportunities?
2. Motivating factors—what encouraged indigenous people to engage in entrepreneurship? Did role models and education play a role?
3. Understand barriers—what barriers did they face? How did they overcome these barriers?
4. Success strategies—what factors led to their success?
5. Growth pathways—how do they intend to grow their enterprise? What are their plans in the future? What is their legacy?

Given that literature on the subject is scarce, the authors conducted interviews to gather first-hand accounts of successful Native American entrepreneurs.

Although complex to structure, the interview selection criteria was fairly simple: (1) The respondent had to be a Native American, (2) he or she had to be presently engaged in an entrepreneurial effort, and (3) the respondent had to be based in the United States.

The interviewees were diverse in terms of age, education, gender, marital status, location, and type of enterprise.

The goal was to gather 20 fully completed interview questionnaires in the time window from May 2018 to May 2019, and this goal was achieved ahead of time.

To the greatest extent possible, the authors sought to gather as many tribes as possible. In the end, only those data were used that were collected from the respondents who completed the questionnaire. In future years, the authors hope to expand the study to cover as many Native American tribes as possible.

Each interview was a unique story of its own. The interviews captured the novel experiences, struggles, and successes of the entrepreneurs. Uniquely, permission was obtained to include each respondent's tribal affiliation. While dissection of this particular data was included within this work, further research should be conducted to gain greater understanding of independent tribal influences and perspectives on entrepreneurship within the United States.

The questionnaire used in this study was originally developed by Dr. J. Mark Munoz and Dr. Michelle Spain. Both authors conducted a previous study on Hispanic Latino and African American entrepreneurs. The authors wish to thank Dr. Michelle Spain for giving her permission to use the questionnaire.

The questions asked were standardized. However, in certain cases, the interviewing author asked follow-up questions to gain added clarity. Personal questions were not asked to respect privacy of the respondents.

It is important to note that Dr. Ron Sheffield, principal investigator of this research, is a member of the Quechan Indian Tribe of Fort Yuma Arizona. While it's impossible for bias not to enter into qualitative research, the authors have made every attempt to only report results of the research questions.

In Table 2.1, the authors list the 15 questions asked and highlight the rationale for each question.

To some degree, the completed questionnaires were adequate. Yet the questions answered opened a floodgate of exciting new angles and ideas for the authors to explore. The authors faced limitations in terms of available resources and the timelines. It is hoped that an expansion of this study may be conducted in the future.

This study captures the psyche of the contemporary Native American entrepreneur. The interviews are groundbreaking and offer unprecedented insights.

Table 2.1 Rationale of the Native American interview questionnaire

Questions	Rationale
Kindly provide an overview of your family history. For example, was there an entrepreneur in your family? Did your family history influence your decision to start a business?	To uncover the extent to which family played a role in Native American entrepreneurship
What was your educational background? Do you have specific views on formal versus informal education? What are your views on Native American entrepreneurial training programs? Has education contributed to your business success?	To understand the role of education in Native American entrepreneurship
Everyone has at least one role model, someone they aspire to be like. Do you have one that is an entrepreneur? How did the role model(s) influence your decision to start a business?	To understand if role models impacted the entrepreneurial decision of the Native American entrepreneur
Starting a new business is not an easy process. What motivated you to start one? What steps did you take to start the business?	To determine what factors influenced the start of an enterprise
What challenges did you face when building your business, and how did you overcome them? Did you come across any unique circumstances as a result of your race?	To examine the barriers and obstacles faced by Native American entrepreneurs and how they overcame these challenges
What types of support were most helpful to you when you were building your business? For example, did your local community play a role in shaping your business interests and development, or maybe it was a mentor? What or who was that one thing that made you believe, "Yes, I can do this!"	To learn the types of support essential for growing Native American enterprises
What do you think are the essential skills needed for Native American entrepreneurs to succeed in America? Also, what personal attitudes do you think are essential?	To uncover skills and attributes necessary for Native American entrepreneurs to succeed
If you had the chance to start over again, would you do anything differently? If so, what's the reason?	To gather insights on mistakes made and lessons learned

(continued)

Questions	Rationale
How would you characterize the state of Native American entrepreneurship in the United States? For instance, is it in the early stages, is it growing, or is it mature? Do you think it is open to all, or limited to certain individuals? Is it viable from anywhere in the country, or more favorable in certain states?	To gain an understanding of the contemporary Native American landscape and viability of locations around the country
Are you a member of business organizations? Are these organizations unique to Native Americans or open to all races? Did they contribute to your business success?	To assess the importance of business organizations in enterprise success
Do you think social networks and personal connections are important to business? Did you use networking when building your business, and are your social networks race based?	To examine the importance of networks and connections in business success
If you could give advice to young Native American entrepreneurs or other young people thinking about starting a business, what would be the most important consideration and why?	To draw additional entrepreneurial insights that might be helpful to the Native American Youth
Have you been involved in socio-civic organizations or philanthropic work? If so, in which organizations, and what role did you play?	To uncover the entrepreneur's level of interest in socio-civic engagements and philanthropy
What do you see happening to your business in the future? Do you have succession plans in place? Do you see your business being run by family members or professional managers, and why?	To gather insights on future planes and extent of forward thinking and succession planning
Where do you see yourself 10 years from now? What do you think is your legacy to the business community?	To determine dreams and aspirations as well as foreseen legacy of Native American entrepreneurs

Note: This questionnaire was designed by Dr. J. Mark Munoz and Dr. Michelle Spain.

Each interview offers a unique and memorable story.

This research study was approved by the Christopher Newport University Institutional Review Board for the protection of human subjects #018.059. The study was conducted by the principal investigator, Dr. Ron Sheffield, formally educated at The George Washington University, and adjunct professor of Leadership and American Studies at CNU in Newport News, Virginia.

The next chapter highlights the interviews and personal journeys of successful Native American entrepreneurs.

CHAPTER 3

Native American Interviews

It does not require many words to speak the truth.
                                    —Chief Joseph, Nez Perce

This section features the full interviews of 20 Native American entrepreneurs from across the United States.

It is important to note that the expressed viewpoints are thoughts and opinions of the interviewee and do not necessarily reflect the thinking of the authors.

These are candid, real-life viewpoints of actual Native American entrepreneurs who practice, or have practiced, their craft on a daily basis.

The authors thank the participants who took time out from their busy schedules to share their viewpoints.

It is hoped that this extensive use of time and effort helps further the understanding and appreciation of Native American entrepreneurship and inspire many to engage in similar pursuits.

The interviews are shown below.

Entrepreneur 1: Tribal Affiliation—Quechan

Question	Response
Kindly provide an overview of your family history. For example, was there an entrepreneur in your family? Did your family history influence your decision to start a business?	I guess you can say my mother. My mom always had this Hustler vibe about her to make sure all of her children were fed and had a roof over our head. Yes, because I saw how hard my mother would work to keep lights on. I told myself, one day I would want to take care of my mother so she would never have to work that hard ever again.
What was your educational background? Do you have specific views on formal versus informal education? What are your views on Native American entrepreneurial training programs? Has education contributed to your business success?	High school and some college. Nope. I feel like tribes should offer some kind of trainings starting with our youth with NAETP because they are our future. Sorry too long of an answer with that. Nope, my drive has.
Everyone has at least one role model, someone they aspire to be like. Do you have one who is an entrepreneur? How did the role model(s) influence your decision to start a business?	A cousin that I met a couple of years ago really lit a fire within myself. His name is [NAME]. Never really meeting another tribal member like him and being my cousin was a bonus! Seeing all his hard work and success drove me to better myself and wanting more in my life for myself.
Starting a new business is not an easy process. What motivated you to start one? What steps did you take to start the business?	My hunger to want more for my children. Sitting down with and pen and paper and writing my ideas down and short-term and long-term goals. From that everything fell into place.
What challenges did you face when building your business, and how did you overcome them? Did you come across any unique circumstances as a result of your race?	Not believing in myself. Pulling up my big girl shorts and kept going. No, not at all.

What types of support were most helpful to you when you were building your business? For example, did your local community play a role in shaping your business interests and development, or maybe it was a mentor? What or who was the one thing that made you believe, "Yes, I can do this!"	Having my children tell me that I was doing a good job and making a difference in people's lives. My drive. Having people that not knowing me saying I helped them and made a difference in their lives.
What do you think are the essential skills needed for Native American entrepreneurs to succeed in America? Also, what personal attitudes do you think are essential?	More support from one's own tribe and funding. Openness to change for the better.
If you had the chance to start over again, would you do anything differently? If so, what's the reason?	No, because everything happens for a reason. Answered that one.
How would you characterize the state of Native American entrepreneurship in the United States? For instance, is it in the early stages, is it growing, or is it mature? Do you think it is open to all, or limited to certain individuals? Is it viable from anywhere in the country, or more favorable in certain states?	Is there any? Not sure. Not sure. Not sure.
Are you a member of business organizations? Are these organizations unique to Native America or open to all races? Did they contribute to your business success?	At the moment, no. At the moment, no. Yes.
Do you think social networks and personal connections are important to business? Did you use networking when building your business, and are your social networks race based?	Yes, as well as Memorandum of understanding (MOU) with other tribes and other agencies in our town and city and off to grow your own business. At first I thought so, but now no because everyone is hit with suicide.
If you could give advice to young Native American entrepreneurs or other young people thinking about starting a business, what would be the most important consideration and why?	You are going to hit some road blocks, when you do breathe and look up to the sky and know your loved ones will give you strength to keep going.

(continued)

Question	Response
Have you been involved in socio-civic organizations or philanthropic work? If so, in which organizations, and what role did you play?	No. No.
What do you see happening to your business in the future? Do you have succession plans in place? Do you see your business being run by family members or professional managers, and why?	Spreading around the world. N/A. My children.
Where do you see yourself 10 years from now? What do you think is your legacy to the business community?	Traveling around the world being a story teller of my life. Saving one life at a time from suicide.

Entrepreneur 2: Tribal Affiliation—Sage, Potawatomi, Delaware

Question	Response
Kindly provide an overview of your family history. For example, was there an entrepreneur in your family? Did your family history influence your decision to start a business?	My grandmother had my mother when she was 15, my mom was pregnant with me at 13, had me at 14. My dad was 15 and was an addict. I chuckled at the question, in that No, I barely had family members with jobs, let alone owning something. I put this down for context to show, if there is a spectrum, my family comes from the side of it that's the furthest from a business owner.
What was your educational background? Do you have specific views on formal versus informal education? What are your views on Native American entrepreneurial training programs? Has education contributed to your business success?	To graduate in San Jose, California you needed 230 credits. At the end of my junior year I had 115 with a .33 GPA that last semester. That was the first time I experienced an "entrepreneur" spirit. I had to buckle down, go to summer school, and college classes, then night school (more college courses during my senior year to catch up). I took the Nike motto "Just Do It" and quit sports, dances, girls, weekends, in the hope I could pull it off. When I graduated, my cake said "Just Did It!" I have never been a part of a formal business educational program, but the way I "fell into" the graduation muscle, I fell into business. The way I had to overcome the odds to graduate, I had to do the same to build my business.

Everyone has at least one role model, someone they aspire to be like. Do you have one who is an entrepreneur? How did the role model(s) influence your decision to start a business?	So, this question threw me. It made me realize, I can't think of one "role model" in the business world. It sounds so shallow as I write it, but I have peers, and things I admire in many people, but I never had a specific person influence this. My influence was always to create a result. When I needed to graduate I didn't have a role model (no one in my family had graduated), but the result of graduating was my influencing factor. Same goes for my business. I was influenced by needing to eat, and live, and found that people would pay me for my gift/services. That slowly turned into a business.
Starting a new business is not an easy process. What motivated you to start one? What steps did you take to start the business?	As I'm sure by now you can tell my road may be weird. I fell into business. I never wanted to be a "business man" suit, briefcase, tie, etc. I never jumped in the Amway or bazillion network marketing, pyramid schemes offered to me since I was 16. I sold Kirby Vacuums at 16, and everyone around me wanted to just be a business man. They got their identity out of whatever title they could get. I've seen countless friends throw thousands of dollars in various network marketing deals to be able to say they are district sales leader, or head of regional sales, you know, go emerald, or diamond, or whatever. I couldn't care less about titles. I did, however, care deeply about the way I connected with people. I did care about people. I did enjoy the art of communication. To communicate where there is influence without manipulation. So while still in my teens I wrote and later recorded music, and eventually found people would pay me to do that. To live though, I had to create something to house me as an artist, and conference facilitator, so I created a business. Got a letter head, created a logo, bank account as a sole prop, later got an EIN # (even though I don't need one.) website etc. Then marketed myself through "word of mouth," over 20 years later . . . ☺

(continued)

Question	Response
What challenges did you face when building your business, and how did you overcome them? Did you come across any unique circumstances as a result of your race?	For starters one challenge is that I am wired for art, reading rooms, and interaction, etc. I LOATHE paperwork! Even a w9 makes me mad. So the first thing I had to overcome was to be professional on the paper side. Contracts, invoices, quotes, receipts, etc., are all counterintuitive for me. But it gets done! It has to! I have actually beat out so many competitors on timely paper work alone. Now race, may need its own page. I know you know, but in case someone else reads this, it's always more than race for tribal people. I see a difference between race and citizenship. Being tribal is navigating both spaces. The unique circumstances based on my tribal background and citizenship is when I try to conduct business with tribes. You would think I have the upper hand, but when it comes to sound and AV, they are more likely (in my experience) to trust a nonnative company for technical assistance than me. I understand all the systemic depravity, and trauma trigger responses, for why, but I deal with that a lot. I also deal with all the white vendors get paid onsite, or early, but they can just mail mine . . . AND (some are coming to me as I am writing). There is a stigma with pricing, unless I'm nonnative. I have heard, "dang guy, trying to charge white guy prices," and then that's who they book ☺ lol. When United or a hotel needs you to put down a deposit they can figure that out, but when I inform them I require a deposit, I'm now only in it for the money.
What types of support were most helpful to you when you were building your business? For example, did your local community play a role in shaping your business interests and development, or maybe it was a mentor? What or who was the one thing that made you believe, "Yes, I can do this!"	I think the organizations that first let me cut my teeth, became that community referenced in the question. But that's it. No tribe money, or assistance. I have had peer mentoring, like Chance and I at different times have been a resource for each other. Early on in my DJing there was a crew that let me set up and tear down so I could practice. I would call a mentor and a role model different, because I did have mentors. But in the end it goes back to results. Results said, "you can do this." ☺

What do you think are the essential skills needed for Native American entrepreneurs to succeed in America? Also, what personal attitudes do you think are essential?	The less colonized we are the more entrepreneurial we could be. Before European contact we were stewards of abundance. Trillions of dollars in natural resources were kept in balance, and traded, and bartered, etc. We had exchanges, so that's in our DNA to be stewards of abundance. The more colonized you are you only do for you, but when you're mindful of the implications outside of you, those value systems, are why I think there are many out there with the upper hand that they don't know they have.
If you had the chance to start over again, would you do anything differently? If so, what's the reason?	Spent way less energy and time on relationships! ☺ I wasn't just off the market, I was out of the market.
How would you characterize the state of Native American entrepreneurship in the United States? For instance, is it in the early stages, is it growing, or is it mature? Do you think it is open to all, or limited to certain individuals? Is it viable from anywhere in the country, or more favorable in certain states?	I have no data. I know that this generation has unprecedented, never-before-on-this-planet opportunity. Eighteen billion dollars is what alcohol companies make on "under age sales!!" Set aside the consumption rates, and just focus on the fact that in that one example kids under 21 have access to unprecedented wealth (if they ever got together) (1) They have access to wealth. (2) They have technology. The computing and production power of the average smart phone . . . but (3) For the first time in recorded history, young people can with one finger send something instantly across the world. So, I don't know what stage we are in, but there's a whole lot of meat on this bone!!
Are you a member of business organizations? Are these organizations unique to Native America or open to all races? Did they contribute to your business success?	Not really a member. Maybe a working relationship. But no contribution other than work. ☺

(continued)

Question	Response
Do you think social networks and personal connections are important to business? Did you use networking when building your business, and are your social networks race based?	See 9. Yes!! Essential!
If you could give advice to young Native American entrepreneurs or other young people thinking about starting a business, what would be the most important consideration and why?	Focus less on starting a business, and more on getting a thing done. Then frame that with business. Pay attention to your credit. You're going to be your only lender for a while. The business makes more sense, when it's how you get what you want done. Find what you LOVE (what you would do for free), gain expertise in it, and then charge a fair price for it. Bam!
Have you been involved in socio-civic organizations or philanthropic work? If so, in which organizations, and what role did you play?	UNITY United National Indian Tribal Youth. I was national rep of my local youth council, co pres, and later National on the National Youth Council where I was voted on the Executive Committee. Now I provide service to the conference in a professional manner. Also AISES and NCAI.
What do you see happening to your business in the future? Do you have succession plans in place? Do you see your business being run by family members or professional managers, and why?	Yes! I am going to move my sole prop over to a NON-Profit structure. I will cap my income, and do less but more impactful outreach. It will later be run by a successor. ☺
Where do you see yourself 10 years from now? What do you think is your legacy to the business community?	Above is the five years, but I would have to talk with my wife about the 10. Ten years ago, I couldn't have imagined I'd be where I am now. So 10 years from now will need to be a "we" answer, not a "me" answer ☺ and my legacy is up to the lips of others. ☺

Entrepreneur 3: Tribal Affiliation—Tsuut'ina

Question	Response
Kindly provide an overview of your family history. For example, was there an entrepreneur in your family? Did your family history influence your decision to start a business?	Both my parents were social workers that owned their own social work practice. I would say that my parents were entrepreneurs growing up. My family had a large impact on why I started my business.
What was your educational background? Do you have specific views on formal versus informal education? What are your views on Native American entrepreneurial training programs? Has education contributed to your business success?	My educational background is in business management and international business. I think it's great to be educated on both sides of the world (native and non-native education). I think this training is essential to the new ways of life. Native people need to be trained on how to make opportunity when there isn't any. I think my education has helped with understanding the overall flow of business, so yes, you could say education has guided me.
Everyone has at least one role model, someone they aspire to be like. Do you have one who is an entrepreneur? How did the role model(s) influence your decision to start a business?	My main role model would have to be my mother; she helped, influenced me to become who I am today. But the real motivator came from my former chief who had a consultant business. A lot of ideas came about after working alongside him.
Starting a new business is not an easy process. What motivated you to start one? What steps did you take to start the business?	The number one thing that inspired me was my little boy; I wanted a better future for him. I began my journey once I had acquired a higher-paying job. It helped me access more funds for my entrepreneurial spirit. I had the mentality to just go out there and start, I would learn along the way. Although I did mess up a lot, overall the experience was worth it.
What challenges did you face when building your business, and how did you overcome them? Did you come across any unique circumstances as a result of your race?	A faced a lot; in fact, I think every day is a new challenge. How I overcame the majority of those challenges was not giving up and quitting. It's very easy to throw in the towel. I developed a strong mentality of, this is it, you have no choice but to go forward and adapt to the situation you have put yourself in. The only thing I came across was the lack of financial knowledge; I am not sure if it is a race thing.

(continued)

Question	Response
What types of support were most helpful to you when you were building your business? For example, did your local community play a role in shaping your business interests and development, or maybe it was a mentor? What or who was the one thing that made you believe, "Yes, I can do this!"	I had help due to leading companies that were geared toward supporting indigenous business. For example, in 2015, I accessed a 25K loan from a loan company that made funds more available to First nation people due to poor or no credit at all. Of course, the interest was a little high but besides that it helped a lot. My community played a role in helping us get off the ground, but they weren't very forgiving if you made a mistake on the job; in fact, they're the reason why I no longer operate on reservations anymore. It's too easy to get chewed up and spit out by them; I prefer to operate off reservation lands. My son and myself were the only things that went through my head when I was going through the trails.
What do you think are the essential skills needed for Native American entrepreneurs to succeed in America? Also, what personal attitudes do you think are essential?	They need to understand that YOU ARE ABLE TO DO WHATEVER YOU WANT AS LONG AS YOU TRY AND GIVE IT YOUR ALL, YOU MUST ADOPT THE MENTALITY OF WOLF THAT NEEDS TO EAT ON THE DAILY AND IS CONSTANTLY LOOKING FOR OPPORTUNITY (food to eat). No shortcuts to success, only more work. You have to unlearn the mentality that the government is looking out for you; they are not looking out for you; it is you and you alone that will be the deciding factor on whether or not you will be great.
If you had the chance to start over again, would you do anything differently? If so, what's the reason?	I would start my business off reservation lands so that I could go through those trails away from home and be better prepared to help the reservation.
How would you characterize the state of Native American entrepreneurship in the United States? For instance, is it in the early stages, is it growing, or is it mature? Do you think it is open to all, or limited to certain individuals? Is it viable from anywhere in the country, or more favorable in certain states?	Entrepreneurship is in its new stages; it needs more time to develop and evolve. It is open to all as long as they know the advantages of their geographical area, native that live in urban areas are at an advantage versus the rural natives, and vice versa, natives who live in rural communities have advantages as well. Its viable in most states, I think a lot has to do with access to capital or leading services within your state.

Question	Response
Are you a member of business organizations? Are these organizations unique to Native Americans or open to all races? Did they contribute to your business success?	I am a proud member of the American Indian Business Leaders; they did contribute to new ventures and opportunities for myself and business. They are open to indigenous people only. They do help me succeed in the business realm.
Do you think social networks and personal connections are important to business? Did you use networking when building your business, and are your social networks race based?	Social networking is extremely important; people rely on this to grow their businesses. I use any element that I could to grow my media production company. My business relies heavily on social networking.
If you could give advice to young Native American entrepreneurs or other young people thinking about starting a business, what would be the most important consideration and why?	Understand your demographics and do your market research. Without these understandings you can't fully get off the ground running.
Have you been involved in socio-civic organizations or philanthropic work? If so, in which organizations, and what role did you play?	I have only been involved with tribal government and a few nonprofits (not sure if that counts toward the question).
What do you see happening to your business in the future? Do you have succession plans in place? Do you see your business being run by family members or professional managers, and why?	I want to be the Native Ted Talk for native people in North America. I have a few plans in place, but they could be worked on and are forever changing as we mature in business. I would like a professional manager who is native, because we need to keep the dollar within our people so they may benefit. I just don't trust my family with running a media production company; I don't think they would know how to make profits.
Where do you see yourself 10 years from now? What do you think is your legacy to the business community?	I would love to have been on council for several terms; I would love to be an economic development advisor or CEO of a tribe/organization. I think by that time I would have several companies owed by me and operating all over the world.

Entrepreneur 4: *Tribal Affiliation—Seminole*

Question	Response
Kindly provide an overview of your family history. For example, was there an entrepreneur in your family? Did your family history influence your decision to start a business?	No, there was not in the current sense—my mother sold items from our home, as well as Seminole skirts, jackets, and sweet grass baskets and dolls.
What was your educational background? Do you have specific views on formal versus informal education? What are your views on Native American entrepreneurial training programs? Has education contributed to your business success?	I graduated from high school. I believe that there are major aspects of education that only life experiences can teach. I love these types of programs and am happy to know that they are available. Yes, education that I have been exposed to via on-the-job training methods.
Everyone has at least one role model, someone they aspire to be like. Do you have one who is an entrepreneur? How did the role model(s) influence your decision to start a business?	N/A
Starting a new business is not an easy process. What motivated you to start one? What steps did you take to start the business?	My mantra has long been "See The Need, Fill The Need," and I clearly saw the need for a company like mine. Writing down my ideas and closely examining my desired objectives, fostering a plan that would allow me to reach the goals as I saw them for the business.
What challenges did you face when building your business, and how did you overcome them? Did you come across any unique circumstances as a result of your race?	Finding the time, as I was employed full time and on call 24/7. I became extremely efficient at compartmentalizing, and sought assistance from trusted associates. No challenges due to my race.
What types of support were most helpful to you when you were building your business? For example, did your local community play a role in shaping your business interests and development, or maybe it was a mentor? What or who was the one thing that made you believe, "Yes, I can do this!"	Having a savings and full-time employment allowed me to have financial stability, which allowed ultimate support. No—primarily, my faith in the Creator gave me the "YES, I CAN" mentality. Secondarily, my mother always felt that and told the world that I could do anything; therefore, I did not want to let her down. Failure was not an option for me.

What do you think are the essential skills needed for Native American entrepreneurs to succeed in America? Also, what personal attitudes do you think are essential?	In my humble opinion, I believe that we must approach our business and its activities not necessarily as a Native American, but as a businessperson. This is not to suggest that we hide or not be proud of our native origin, simply that business must be kept at the forefront. A positive attitude, willingness to learn and teach, as well as accepting that we are not always the expert and that there are many that we can learn from.
If you had the chance to start over again, would you do anything differently? If so, what's the reason?	Yes, I would have engaged the SBA and the many organizations that exist for funding. I exhausted much of my own financial resources, whereby I could have applied for and was eligible for financial assistance. I just did not know about them.
How would you characterize the state of Native American entrepreneurship in the United States? For instance, is it in the early stages, is it growing, or is it mature? Do you think it is open to all, or limited to certain individuals? Is it viable from anywhere in the country, or more favorable in certain states?	I would say that the current timing is tremendous for all those not just natives, seeking to be entrepreneurs. I believe that the opportunity for anyone that is committed to be in business is possible, much to do with the state of technology, today.
Are you a member of business organizations? Are these organizations unique to Native Americans or open to all races? Did they contribute to your business success?	Yes. They are open to all people. No.
Do you think social networks and personal connections are important to business? Did you use networking when building your business, and are your social networks race based?	Yes, relationships are very important and the way in which we present ourselves. No and No.
If you could give advice to young Native American entrepreneurs or other young people thinking about starting a business, what would be the most important consideration and why?	I would recommend that one educate themselves on the direction in which they would want to go in—not take for granted that they know everything, take the time to research and research some more.
Have you been involved in socio-civic organizations or philanthropic work? If so, in which organizations, and what role did you play?	Yes. Professional growth for women in business as an educator sharing best practices.

(continued)

Question	Response
What do you see happening to your business in the future? Do you have succession plans in place? Do you see your business being run by family members or professional managers, and why?	I see my business growing successfully rapidly. I am working on a succession plan, as I believe in the importance of them, yet have not made the time to execute one. Both, because the day-to-day operation of the business will require someone that is highly knowledgeable of the profession and the professional world beyond family ties. Family in an effort to keep the vision alive and eventually allow them to lead the business with benchmarks in place.
Where do you see yourself 10 years from now? What do you think is your legacy to the business community?	Being a viable business in the world today and in the future. Establishing franchises of the model company that has been created. The legacy of no matter who you are, or where you have come from, success is always possible if you are willing to be diligent.

Entrepreneur 5: Tribal Affiliation—Mohican, Delaware

Question	Response
Kindly provide an overview of your family history. For example, was there an entrepreneur in your family? Did your family history influence your decision to start a business?	My family history is Polish and Muncy, which is Mohican in Delaware. And as far as I can go back we've gone back seven generations, but at least in the most recent three generations there have been entrepreneurs. My father was a logger. My grandfather and my great grandfather Bopara were loggers too and did it impact me.
	I guess I never—I didn't consciously go into being an entrepreneur. Knowing that I had entrepreneurs in my family but certainly providing for your family working hard and you know doing something you're passionate about and that you're leading was of great interest to me. I worked for public education agencies at the local or state level for quite a while or at university level and then due to work circumstances ended up starting my own business in 2000 and won. And it's been going good ever since. What is your educational background? I have a bachelor's degree in elementary education, a master's degree in curriculum and instruction, and a doctorate, a PhD from the University of Wisconsin Madison.

What was your educational background? Do you have specific views on formal versus informal education? What are your views on Native American entrepreneurial training programs? Has education contributed to your business success?	There aren't many Native American academics. I feel that if you are in trades or manufacturing or even finance or banking there are a lot more curriculum and things available, but in terms of my formal training that would help me out with a policy leadership governance not too much. There's a little bit down at the University of Arizona, but that's more for a tribal nation.
	Elected leaders they don't have a lot caring for indigenous academics who are interested in culture sovereignty policy and researcher evaluations. So, it's rough but you know you kind of figure out what is going, you know. Feel happy when things are in season; when they don't you just go back to the drawing board and you know figure it out so you can be an effective and responsive entrepreneur. So far so good; 20 years right in terms of success. How has education contributed to your business success greatly? So I get informal education through culture language camps doing ceremonies and just being a good traditional community member.
	And so you know you're doing well when you are given teachings the eagle fathers are regalia sacred responsibilities.
	They give me blessings on my academic and professional work that I do. And then on the other hand if you look at my formal education within the Western world or academic or policy context you have to count it didn't matter; so I used the colonial tools to dismantle the colonial Hall so that sovereignty culture and community are able to have a voice again.
	So I use for my education as medicine to try to get our voices back and hopefully some of our rights as well.

(continued)

Question	Response
Everyone has at least one role model, someone they aspire to be like. Do you have one who is an entrepreneur? How did the role model(s) influence your decision to start a business?	I don't know many indigenous academic entrepreneurs. They work for state or federal agencies. There are many indigenous academics that I look up to. But in terms of being entrepreneurial my inspiration comes from my family, because of more years they were entrepreneurs. Concurrently, I was also doing family and historical research. You know as I learned about who I was, where it came from, what they did, and I'm just really proud because I think through the generations of [family name] you can really see how we worked hard and we had cultural and professional humility. We were very giving and worked in service to others, including our families, and we were generous people, and we always dress good. So I feel like we are a good look into where we were leading and doing our work. That's a little bit of a joke, but you know there's a lot of pride in doing that. And so my [family name] men were the folks that I looked up to.
Starting a new business is not an easy process. What motivated you to start one? What steps did you take to start the business?	Yes, I was motivated because I was not employed. My job had ended at the state education agency that I worked for. And frankly they weren't addressing the needs of tribal nations or tribal communities or families anyway. So it was a blessing in disguise. And what steps to take survival is just get out there, work hard to get it done. The contacts that I had made in public agencies had been caring, generous, and authentically hard working, follow-through with details, effective and responsive to needs, and community and culture and so on.

	I just feel as though they knew me for that good reputation, trustworthy hard working. And so I just took that I took those skill sets in those networks into my entrepreneurial life, and some of my first contracts are with school districts or agencies that I had worked for under my public life. And so those were kind of the steps and then I just took you know one month at a time, one year at a time, and I can't believe it's been 20 years.
What challenges did you face when building your business, and how did you overcome them? Did you come across any unique circumstances as a result of your race?	So we started out small and weak; that was one challenge when we started in the basement of my home, and we were like turtles; the growth was slow but steady. And as we got bigger we were able to get our own building. We just rent. I think one of the biggest challenges is figuring out from a capacity issue what your organization can handle, what they're good at. I feel like I've always have had a natural tendency to be flexible with whatever the market needs were. Even though I don't have any formal MBA or other business training you know; I listened and I was responsive.
	You know, I guess I got that from my childhood because you had to listen and be responsive where or you'd get a willow stick. So that was a good lesson I learned. And then another challenge was learning how to be comfortable with making a profit because in many indigenous communities money is seen as evil or as a tool for greed or acting better than others.
	We weren't raised that way, but it has allowed some people in my organization to get too close to my banking. And I was embezzled from a cousin who had worked for me and that was a one-time only but it was you know a fifty-thousand dollar mistake, and I didn't go bankrupt. I went back to my roots of working hard, having humility, and one of the most challenging times in my life.

(continued)

Question	Response
	It was one of the very best teachers in terms of my relationship with money help business operations work how to tighten up financial controls and administrative oversight.
	And it has made operations run smoother. And we've also learned that we don't need to carry 20 or 30 projects and try to be a multimillion dollar company. It's much more comfortable in my life to bring in you know five-, six-, eight-hundred-thousand dollars annually in revenue and just be more profitable and keep the number of projects down to 8 to 10 or 12 and keep the staff small and you know use consultants if you need some Ph.D.s. These are subject matter experts and so that that's kind of how the challenges have been teachers.
	You know you just had to have like put your pride aside and have humility to be open to that. If any of those challenges come because of your race, well I mean, I think because I have a Polish mom and a native that people can't readily tell. But I mean I've gotten certifications and different things for being female minority status native status. And sometimes you know, sometimes your own community like native members don't want to count you or have you be part of programming and things because maybe you don't live on the reservation or back in the community or there might be kind of the crab-in-the-bucket syndrome but because of my traditional teachings, you know, you don't, you don't clap back, you just, you have humility in the work that you do and in the profit that you make and you give back can you do sponsorships not everything with your name on it and you just kind of you know life gives you lessons and you kind of learn how to deal with it.

What types of support were most helpful to you when you were building your business? For example, did your local community play a role in shaping your business interests and development, or maybe it was a mentor? What or who was the one thing that made you believe, "Yes, I can do this!"	Yes, I do this, I had a good family, and I think I was born with the best I can do just hard work and belief in self. I had a lot of success in school and in academics from early on. I was all about performance. I could run faster than the boys I was better at sports than most all of them even through high school. And so this need to perform and be effective was reinforced that early age. I think that, yes, there were mentors along the way, but some of the most helpful things were just having nonnative people open the door and say OK let's talk about your business line of credit.
	And they talked to me as a business person and as a female novice native there are a lot of native and nonnative people who opened the door for tribes tribal organizations or public or foundation agencies to allow me to have contracts or be in schools to be to be a consultant. And if I did good work that you know that's pretty much all that mattered.
	Other helpful ness was I had a really good husband and family that supported me CPA who came in and reconcile my books every month to make sure I didn't mess anything up. But [Name] my CPA is still with me to this day and I think the people that I had in my immediate circle are still around an attorney who is always a good person to have and I have a good attorney that knows tribal law and public law and case law and both of those contacts and people who understood my passion and my vision and my sense of humor so culture and language were good things for me to have because.
	And then my formal education braided together made the PC for what's this I'm passionate in love, culture, language, community, and sovereignty. I just didn't realize that my formal education in policy research and evaluation would lend itself to me being an entrepreneur and having a successful business that is able to support many native and nonnative families and causes that once you see the essential skills for Native American entrepreneurs in America.

(continued)

Question	Response
What do you think are the essential skills needed for Native American entrepreneurs to succeed in America? Also, what personal attitudes do you think are essential?	Well, first of all, I think that you need to have business skills regardless of your race or ethnicity or gender or whatever intersectionality you have got. That being said those are things that you learn externally. Right. And so if you have a core that is terms of Native American it's you know your traditional teachings and you have elders that you can go to and speak with as well as some of those traditional teachers who have college degrees or life experiences. And being in economic development business or entrepreneurial ventures is important because their traditional teachings are the cultural grounding that she needs not only to run your business with the ups and downs but also gives you the courage to speak back to the traditional training curriculum tax technical assistance services you get to say this is great for a Western context. But what would it mean for an indigenous context or a Native American entrepreneur? It allowed me my traditional content knowledge allowed me to be able to speak back to the University of Wisconsin Madison. But how would we do it for tribal nations indigenous context tribal community members living on the rez. So I between my traditional knowledge of the core and then getting formal education I was able to have the confidence and the competencies you know to really forge a new path and the way we do work and that's not only been helpful to me and the indigenous community but it's really helped that academic and policy community as well expand their awareness and their capacities and their responses.

If you had the chance to start over again, would you do anything differently? If so, what's the reason?	I think that I would have worked or tried to be formal or informal mentee to a Native American academic consulting organization. I would have been in a mentor protégé program like you see at the federal level. I wish more tribes had mentor protégé programs in college call it being a good and you're being a good uncle. But I wish there were more programs like that formally where firms like tribal tech or Kaufman and Associates would be mentors to new and emerging indigenous policy research evaluation firms. I wish I would have had more time. But you know when you're unemployed you just have to get out and go to work. So that's what I did. So looking back if I . . . if I had a choice now knowing what I know that's what I have done, I would have, I would have been mentored, I would have had a formal mentor.
How would you characterize the state of Native American entrepreneurship in the United States? For instance, is it in the early stages, is it growing, or is it mature? Do you think it is open to all, or limited to certain individuals? Is it viable from anywhere in the country, or more favorable in certain states?	So I don't know if I'm native entrepreneurship is good or not. But I'll let the researcher of the study figure that out as part of their literature review. From what I can tell I don't see it in my small circle. I don't see it growing. I don't see many of us lasting. I think that good isn't the only model that should be used to measure entrepreneurs. Because some of us stated earlier on purpose choose to have small firms. For many life–work balance reasons to have a bigger impact for the smaller number of areas that we're trying to have impact in in terms of locality. You almost have to be in Washington, D.C. or a beltway bandit to get that work. I think that it's limiting because the people who get contracts most of the time aren't necessarily the highest qualified people. They're just the ones who are most known to the pyramid officers who are putting the contracts out there. They certainly aren't the most culturally responsive or effective that way.

(continued)

Question	Response
	If they weren't, then the outcomes for these various studies and initiatives would be changing over the last 80 to 100 years. And they haven't point cases because look at education and education in our social or our economic or our human services. You know health outcomes haven't changed much. That means that people at the state and federal government or foundations are hiring to do the studies they need to have. For me, indigenous people and indigenous contractors working collaboratively with the prime contractor because there needs to be cultural competency not just shoving Western model on tribal nations and tribal communities it's not working. Like I said, if it was the outcome data would be different in it's not in terms of sole locality matters.
	It also matters to your networks if you're not rich and you can't live in the beltway of your state or of the nation's capital or contribute high dollars to the two campaigns that are giving out the contracts.
	Producing good work being effective working at or under budget. And you know always having to be careful to protect your intellectual property because there are a lot of native and nonnative organizations a lot of nonnative that will work with feel but then they work with you one time and the feel of your work and then go out and work on you know national contracts. So you know it's a constant battle that's for sure. Absolutely. Keep your guard up.

Are you a member of business organizations? Are these organizations unique to Native Americans or open to all races? Did they contribute to your business success?	Yes, I belong to you know the local Chamber of Commerce, the Chamber of Commerce the state, and the Chamber of Commerce all Minority Business Development Agency for the state.
	We need more laws and implementation of those laws and evaluating the effectiveness of those laws because there's a lot of tribal nations that will hire white firms before they hire native firms.
	You know where they don't have laws in place so they've got the law in place but they don't have policy process to implement it consistently across their tribal departments. I also think that there are limits because of these organizations that I belong to Chambers of Commerce want to focus on easy stuff like retail and if you belong to any other chambers you know where minority business development agencies they focus on manufacturing and trade. So I feel because of the disciplinary that I'm in with quality research and evaluation and technical assistance around that we're carrying on a strategic studies or strategic plans.
	There is a . . . the business agencies do not. They don't even set up networking events where my academic agency can have speed dates with other agencies that are buying studies or wanting training or technical assistance. You know they don't get; it doesn't happen. So they stick more to trade manufacturing roads and highways and you know maybe that's service industry or retail industry.

Question	Response
Do you think social networks and personal connections are important to business? Did you use networking when building your business, and are your social networks race based?	I have tried to answer your question yes and you should have heard throughout the last 20 minutes that this social academic and native networks are critically important and there are places to partner in to showcase my work and how effective our work products and our services are. I do have purposeful and intentional networks. Some are race based some aren't. But if I'm working with nonnative organizations who wanting to increase their capacity and effectiveness working with tribal nations and commune tribal communities then you have to have some race great targeters or if you will have networks of social networks academic networks. And frankly, I have to, because if I only relied on Western education or Western academic networks I would be content information to help me with indigenous theory policy practice. We're the ones creating that intellectual property and that information and so it doesn't come from Western networks; it comes from indigenous people and indigenous networks young Native Americans. The most important consideration is don't feel entitled. I work hard to figure out how traditional language and knowledge can be applied to Western initiatives and projects. Figure out how to build bridges. Be authentic, be hard working and be sober and be humble.
If you could give advice to young Native American entrepreneurs or other young people thinking about starting a business, what would be the most important consideration and why?	The most important consideration is don't feel entitled work hard look at. Figure out how your traditional language and knowledge can be applied to Western initiatives and projects. Figure out how to build bridges. Be authentic, be hard working and be sober and be humble.

Have you been involved in socio-civic organizations or philanthropic work? If so, in which organizations, and what role did you play?	I work with many philanthropic and social. Socio-civic could mean civic organizations with a social justice mission and nonprofits.
	We native and nonnatives help build capacity, we build systems studies, we build systems infrastructure for comprehensive consistent and systemic data collection across programs divisions in the organization itself to see its mission and vision are being met. To see a program in divisionary metrics are being met. We've worked with grantees to help them understand the evaluation and use data as a strategy for communicating not only impact but value to their various stakeholders. We've worked nationally across organizations and states and tribal nations so that there is consistent data collection across 50 states that have youth councils or you know there's consistent data collection between tribal and tribal health and human service organizations when studying tribal opioid or opioid addiction generally in a particular state.
	And so yeah we've worked with a lot of different organizations, and I believe that the special the foundation are really interested in helping in not only building their own capacity but culturally responsive policy research evaluation, but they are particularly interested in the grantees. They give money to developing in those areas as well and how tribal nations and tribal communities can use the valuation as medicine to communicate in culturally responsive ways through Photo Voice storytelling digital storytelling oral history. How do you combine that with the more Western notions of evaluation and research.
	So we do. We're going to be working with the Kellogg Foundation Northwest Area Foundation Noble Foundation. I mean there's lots of different authorities to drag it out.

(*continued*)

Question	Response
What do you see happening to your business in the future? Do you have succession plans in place? Do you see your business being run by family members or professional managers, and why?	I'm 47, so I imagine I'll be working another 20 or 30 years. I can't see. You know when I retire I'll have some kind of you know 3- to 5-year clothes plan. But at some level I've always been at my organization open because it's an academic you can see you can be writing or other work you know quarterly or monthly you know up until you can't walk anymore. I guess they could roll me in on a wheelchair which could say the academic work into their 70s and 80s.

So I'm going to be working while I like it very much. I like the freedom of being an entrepreneur, and I also like the tax benefits that you get and also my hourly rate is way better here than working for a public university or other agencies. So I don't have a succession plan and I don't have kids so I'm not one of my nieces nephews. They want to run it great or if there was a friend or another organization who I could trust you know maybe I would maybe I would sell it.

But it's you know I'll just my projects are anywhere from three to two years so I'll just stop doing projects all gracefully project out and go gently into the night.

All right well last question on the future. Where do you see yourself 10 years from now? You know said what 20 to 30 years from now and what do you think is your legacy to the business community. Where are you 10 years from now? What is your legacy? Ten or 10 years from now.

I'm making $300 an hour. I'll be in the prime of my academic life. I mean my PhD is just three years old. So I look at myself with three years old. So I will be doing keynotes all around the world for native and nonnative organizations. Hopefully I'll be continuing to mentor more and more young evaluators. I've sort of started that now I'll have more staff around me that will be taking leadership roles leading or cold leading studies that are indigenous. And let's see the legacy that I want to leave with I want to be a good [Name] I want to I want to. |

	It's important for me to raise up aspiring evaluators or academics people you know even I don't really want to mentor entrepreneurs unless they're going to be "entrepreneuring" in the field of academia because we are not in the Western literature and we were in many of most of the disciplines that we need to have indigenous scholarship that is grounded in culture, language, and community. That's how you walk that humility and balance as an entrepreneur you have to be connected to communities. They can always keep you in check. You have to know your teaching and how you apply that to whatever discipline or craft that you have.
Where do you see yourself 10 years from now? What do you think is your legacy to the business community?	So my legacy is to have you know maybe in 10 years the book I'll have written for sure a bunch of articles you know 10 or 20 articles that will help inform the future generation. You know folks from Western content and how you do work but also that's infused with traditional knowledge and I and I heard one comment at this last conference the American devaluation association was that that really made me think about the impact that I'm having because you know sometimes you write me work in isolation you don't know traditional Alaskan native woman came up to me and she works for an Alaskan native organization that does policy research and evaluation, and she came up to me at this conference in November and said Dr. [Name] I've always you know I read everything here blogs and everything you put out your articles. And she said if all you publish in your traditional name what you [in audible] she always wanted to do that my boss wouldn't let me. So this year I brought in all your articles and I said to Dr. [Name] to do it why can't I so she said if Dr. [Name] could do it why can't I.

(continued)

Question	Response
	And that was like one of the biggest compliments you know so knowing their culture and language and then you awaken what your ancestors are doing in a good way. You know we need paychecks because we support families in need of initiatives or domestic violence in this which is super important.
Author an academic in a traditional impact and you're showing them how your elders' knowledge is timeless and can be applied to anything including publishing in your indigenous name. But the contact there in or the training or whatever is like that's helping me lift my spirits name. So that's like that's like one of the best compliments that I've gotten ever in my whatever.
Twenty-five plus year career. So, I guess that's a good way to go.
Thank you Dr. [Name] for your hard work and I look forward to your legacy.

Entrepreneur 6: Tribal Affiliation—Quechan

Question	Response
Kindly provide an overview of your family history. For example, was there an entrepreneur in your family? Did your family history influence your decision to start a business?	My dad was an entrepreneur from a young age. From what I can remember he was always starting businesses every few years. My mom would always support him and would be the other half of the business. My mom is also an entrepreneur and opened her own business when she was a bit older and we were grown up. I think it is engrained in me to be an entrepreneur. My brain is just wired that way, but it makes it a lot easier to have confidence to do it since I was able to watch my parents do it. It obviously was never easy, but my parents pulled it off and came out for the better because of their decisions.

What was your educational background? Do you have specific views on formal versus informal education? What are your views on Native American entrepreneurial training programs? Has education contributed to your business success?	I have a bachelor's degree in international affairs from George Mason University (GMU) and a master's degree in gender and sexuality studies from George Washington University. Getting a formal education was not an option for me growing up as my parents are both educators in the university system and both had PhDs. I strongly believe that a formal education is the key to success as it opens many doors that likely would not exist had you not attended a formal university. Native American entrepreneurial training programs would be super beneficial, and I don't think enough exist in Indian Country. I have never attended one but would love to if it was in my area. Education has 100% contributed to my success. I don't think I would be where I am today financially, professionally, or personally had I not had the education I did.
Everyone has at least one role model, someone they aspire to be like. Do you have one who is an entrepreneur? How did the role model(s) influence your decision to start a business?	Yes, my dad is my role model. He has opened and operated several businesses and has had no fear in doing so. It was amazing to watch such confidence growing up because I now have that same confidence to do the same thing. I think a big part about having the confidence to do something is to watch someone close to you do that very thing and succeed.
Starting a new business is not an easy process. What motivated you to start one? What steps did you take to start the business?	I saw an area that needed improvement in Indian Country and I just decided to do it. I saw that native youth needed access to opportunities that would further their lives in all ways, so along with my boss, started a program to help Native American youth in business. The steps I took to start it were asking folks in the community what would help native students most and trying to make sure we included that in our program. We got a federal grant to implement an internship program specifically for Native American youth so I just started from scratch and built out a program. The first year was a ton of work, but this year I'm building off of what I did last year and making it even better.

(continued)

Question	Response
What challenges did you face when building your business, and how did you overcome them? Did you come across any unique circumstances as a result of your race?	It was a ton of work. It was hard to balance my personal and professional lives. A lot of times my husband would ask me to stop working so late so that I could spend time with him. It was hard to pull away from my work because I'm so passionate about it. I am getting better at this so I don't burn myself out and let down those in my personal life by trying to work between a core set of hours like 9 a.m. to 5 p.m. or 10 a.m. to 6 p.m. to make sure I'm not neglecting my own health and personal life. I don't feel like I came across any particular obstacles because of my race (at least in this particular instance) since I am working within Indian Country. If anything, my race helped me in this instance.
What types of support were most helpful to you when you were building your business? For example, did your local community play a role in shaping your business interests and development, or maybe it was a mentor? What or who was the one thing that made you believe, "Yes, I can do this!"	My boss played a huge role in starting this project. She is great to bounce ideas off of and will let me know if a particular idea I have is too grandiose or far-fetched. She is the most motivating mentor I could have.
What do you think are the essential skills needed for Native American entrepreneurs to succeed in America? Also, what personal attitudes do you think are essential?	I think essential skills for Native American entrepreneurs to have to succeed in the United States are a) formal education and b) the ability to live in two worlds. Having a formal education is essential because it is the way of the "white man." The only way an indigenous-owned business will be acknowledged and eventually successful is to speak the same language as mainstream society. It is an unfortunate reality since Native Americans were violently forced throughout history to assimilate to colonial society, but that is the way it is now. Formal education is one of those ways you can speak the same language and be on the same playing field. It is essential that a Native American entrepreneur be able to live in two worlds because they will have to succeed.

	Most native people hold their culture close to them and it plays a huge role in their identity. Most native values and goals will differ from those of business within the dominant culture. Bridging the gap between your values and the values of the mainstream business world is essential for success. Personal attitudes that are important for success are definitely confidence and reliance. These may apply for all entrepreneurs despite your race, but they are of utmost importance for native entrepreneurs. Taking into consideration historical impacts to native communities and, composing less than 2 percent of the population, native entrepreneurs will have several unique hurdles in front of them when they set out to start a business. The ability to stay strong and know that you will succeed no matter how many times you fail is essential for success.
If you had the chance to start over again, would you do anything differently? If so, what's the reason?	I don't believe so. Everything I have done has led me to where I am today.
How would you characterize the state of Native American entrepreneurship in the United States? For instance, is it in the early stages, is it growing, or is it mature? Do you think it is open to all, or limited to certain individuals? Is it viable from anywhere in the country, or more favorable in certain states?	It is certainly in the early stages. I don't think many people know how to even find Native American–owned businesses. I think it is open to all, but it is certainly more prevalent in the West and Midwest since there is a higher concentration of tribal communities and more knowledge around Native American cultures.
Are you a member of business organizations? Are these organizations unique to Native Americans or open to all races? Did they contribute to your business success?	I am not.
Do you think social networks and personal connections are important to business? Did you use networking when building your business, and are your social networks race based?	Social networks are absolutely important for business success. I believe that without them, achieving success would be 10 times harder. I found the position I'm in now through my father who sits on the board of the organization I work for. My social networks are not race based. I have social connections across all races and identities.

(continued)

Question	Response
If you could give advice to young Native American entrepreneurs or other young people thinking about starting a business, what would be the most important consideration and why?	Don't be afraid to fail. One thing I have learned about entrepreneurship is to dream big and you might not always succeed, but if you don't, you can always try again. I think it comes from growing up with parents who lived in poverty. They always told me that they knew what rock bottom looked like and the worst that could happen was that they'd end up back there, but the best thing that could happen was that they knew they would succeed. They weren't scared of failing because they knew they were capable of climbing out of it like they had with poverty.
Have you been involved in socio-civic organizations or philanthropic work? If so, in which organizations, and what role did you play?	Yes, I work for the National American Indian Business Leaders as the associate executive director. I helped start a brand new project that helps indigenous youth follow their dreams through business opportunities and interpleural education.
What do you see happening to your business in the future? Do you have succession plans in place? Do you see your business being run by family members or professional managers, and why?	I see our business growing and thriving. Me and my team have so many amazing ideas that will not only allow us to succeed, but the communities we serve, indigenous youth and entrepreneurs. I do not have a succession plan in place at (at least for the moment as I don't see myself ever transitioning out of this role (at least for the foreseeable future). I think the business will be run by professional managers since I don't believe any of my family members will want my job. We all work in quite different fields and levels.
Where do you see yourself 10 years from now? What do you think is your legacy to the business community?	It's hard to imagine where I will be in 10 years. If I had to guess, I'd say I will be way more well-versed in how to operate a business and how to start a new one. I imagine I will have another business where I am doing something a little more personal a.k.a. something more akin to my hobbies and personal life. Likely, this will be in addition to another job still in the realm of indigenous youth education since that is my passion.

Entrepreneur 7: Tribal Affiliation—Navajo

Question	Response
Kindly provide an overview of your family history. For example, was there an entrepreneur in your family? Did your family history influence your decision to start a business?	My younger sister and I grew up in an abusive household (my father abused my mother) until I was 10 years old when my parents finally separated. My mother and father both worked service/customer service–oriented jobs and the only narrative I heard was, we didn't have enough and that is was the white man's fault. This was mostly portrayed through my father. So, now, there were no entrepreneurs in my family, and growing up poor definitely put a great desire in my heart to better my life on my own.
What was your educational background? Do you have specific views on formal versus informal education? What are your views on Native American entrepreneurial training programs? Has education contributed to your business success?	I have a bachelor's degree in accounting. I started my MBA in 2010 but never finished it. I have been making plans to go back to school to finish it by 2020. I believe in education, but do not believe it is required to become successful. I love the fact that there are entrepreneurial training programs. I see so many natives who use their natural talents to monetize off of, yet they lack basic business fundamentals which are critical to growing as an entrepreneur. I wouldn't say education has directly contributed to my success. However, in my industry, we have to be professionally licensed to do what we do, so yes, obtaining those professional licenses has definitely helped me stand out as a financial advisor and bring a wealth of knowledge to my clients and my practice.
Everyone has at least one role model, someone they aspire to be like. Do you have one who is an entrepreneur? How did the role model(s) influence your decision to start a business?	My role model is [Name] aka Litefoot. He is a Cherokee business owner that started out as a rapper. I've watched his career since I was a young teenager and have definitely appreciated his growth into the business man that he is today. I wouldn't say he influenced me to start a business though.

(continued)

Question	Response
Starting a new business is not an easy process. What motivated you to start one? What steps did you take to start the business?	When I first got into my industry, I worked as an assistant to a few very successful financial advisors. Over time, watching them manage their practices, I thought to myself "Why can't I do what they do on my own?" My motivation was to work for my community (black/brown/natives) and offer financial services to them, because very few financial advisors cared to work in that market. That's when I first incorporated. From there I found the best platform to use as my back office to start my own practice. It was actually an easy process.
What challenges did you face when building your business, and how did you overcome them? Did you come across any unique circumstances as a result of your race?	Ha, my biggest challenge and still is my biggest challenge is marketing to my target market. Over time as my skillset and knowledge increased, so has my desire to work with more affluent individuals. I'm working to overcome that challenge by building strategic partnerships and developing a marketing model that pretty much uses content I created on my own.
What types of support were most helpful to you when you were building your business? For example, did your local community play a role in shaping your business interests and development, or maybe it was a mentor? What or who was the one thing that made you believe, "Yes, I can do this!"	My family was my biggest support. My mother in particular always believed in my dreams and motivated to continue on when I became discouraged. What made me believe I could do this was after meeting with a few new clients to work with that were not family members and them being extremely grateful to work with me and to use my services. I was like "OK, I must be doing something right!"
What do you think are the essential skills needed for Native American entrepreneurs to succeed in America? Also, what personal attitudes do you think are essential?	I think the first is networking. Being willing to network outside your tribe, comfort zone, etc. Also, not depending on your tribe or others to do something for you. Personal attitudes would also be confidence, resilience, and skillset.

Question	Response
If you had the chance to start over again, would you do anything differently? If so, what's the reason?	Yes, I would put more value on my work versus marketing myself as a commodity. I would definitely have charge for my time. I'm just now figuring how to build consultation fees (compliantly) into my practice because I'm so used to being the one that gives everything away and does a lot for free. I've learned the hard way, that doesn't attract the type of clientele I really want to work with.
How would you characterize the state of Native American entrepreneurship in the United States? For instance, is it in the early stages, is it growing, or is it mature? Do you think it is open to all, or limited to certain individuals? Is it viable from anywhere in the country, or more favorable in certain states?	I believe Native American (NA)entrepreneurship is definitely growing. I wouldn't say so much in infancy stages but just now spreading. I think more natives are becoming and believing they can be entrepreneurs. I do believe it is open to all and not more viable in one place versus another. This country was built on capitalism, and I believe anyone from anywhere can come up with a solution to a problem everyone has and build a business doing so.
Are you a member of business organizations? Are these organizations unique to Native Americans or open to all races? Did they contribute to your business success?	I just became a member of the Native American Chamber of Commerce of Illinois. It just started this month, so no I have not benefited just yet.
Do you think social networks and personal connections are important to business? Did you use networking when building your business, and are your social networks race based?	I believe personal connections are more beneficial than social networking. Networking these days is just a thing, everyone does it, and very rarely do you walk away with any meaningful connections. No, I did not use social networking to build my business. And the ones I used to try to go to were not race based.
If you could give advice to young Native American entrepreneurs or other young people thinking about starting a business, what would be the most important consideration and why?	My focus on helping young entrepreneurs would be helping them determine what problem in the world are you solving? How dedicated are you to legitimizing this business? What personal and professional skills would you continue to develop? I know these are questions, but these are the things I would advise on.

(continued)

Question	Response
Have you been involved in socio-civic organizations or philanthropic work? If so, in which organizations, and what role did you play?	Honestly, not really involved. I have attended a few meetings with some nonprofits but have not chosen to personally get involved. I am passionate about working with union organizations and am currently seeking to become treasurer of the Chicago Women in Trades organization.
What do you see happening to your business in the future? Do you have succession plans in place? Do you see your business being run by family members or professional managers, and why?	I plan to grow my team to a minimum of 10 financial advisors who operate at my capacity with full staff running my office. I do have a succession plan in place, in which my mother would receive residual income from my current clientele and later once my daughter turns 18, she could take over my business if she chooses to.
Where do you see yourself 10 years from now? What do you think is your legacy to the business community?	10 years from now, I see myself being the first Native American woman in my industry to be a million-dollar income earner. ☺

Entrepreneur 8: Tribal Affiliation—Ho-Chunk

Question	Response
Kindly provide an overview of your family history. For example, was there an entrepreneur in your family? Did your family history influence your decision to start a business?	I am a tribal member of the Ho-Chunk Nation, Black River Falls, my mother's great grandmother was [Name], the first Native American to earn a medical degree, she was a tribal member of the Omaha Nation. My family history did not influence my decision to start a business.
What was your educational background? Do you have specific views on formal versus informal education? What are your views on Native American entrepreneurial training programs? Has education contributed to your business success?	Administrative Assistant, Casino Management. Prefer formal education over informal. I support Native American entrepreneurial training program; I have completed one and received a loan upon completion. Yes, education has very much contributed to my business success.

Question	Response
Everyone has at least one role model, someone they aspire to be like. Do you have one who is an entrepreneur? How did the role model(s) influence your decision to start a business?	No, my role model was not an entrepreneur.
Starting a new business is not an easy process. What motivated you to start one? What steps did you take to start the business?	I watched my best friend who had no education run and operate a roofing installation company, I watch him and started my own. I then took all the steps, starting with incorporating.
What challenges did you face when building your business, and how did you overcome them? Did you come across any unique circumstances as a result of your race?	First challenge was too much competition. The best would survive; being Native American, I knew I had to do and be a better company. I came up with a great marketing plan and it worked; won entrepreneur of the year two times; that sure helped. At that point, race was not a factor.
What types of support were most helpful to you when you were building your business? For example, did your local community play a role in shaping your business interests and development, or maybe it was a mentor? What or who was the one thing that made you believe, "Yes, I can do this!"	Support was becoming a board of director at nonprofit organizations, joining the local Rotary club, and the American Indian Chamber of Commerce of Minnesota, Minneapolis Chamber of Commerce, St. Paul Chamber of Commerce, and the Twin Cities Leadership course sponsored by the Minneapolis Chamber of Commerce.
What do you think are the essential skills needed for Native American entrepreneurs to succeed in America? Also, what personal attitudes do you think are essential?	Having a business mentor is essential, as many as you can find. You must learn how to sell yourself.
If you had the chance to start over again, would you do anything differently? If so, what's the reason?	Never buy a yellow page ad ever again. They don't work.
How would you characterize the state of Native American entrepreneurship in the United States? For instance, is it in the early stages, is it growing, or is it mature? Do you think it is open to all, or limited to certain individuals? Is it viable from anywhere in the country, or more favorable in certain states?	The state of Native American entrepreneurship could use more support from their tribal nation for sure. "Indian buy Indian" is what they say, but they don't support that! There could be more done to teach our children early about entrepreneurship as well also. Open to all for sure, but more classes about entrepreneurship would help. Some states and tribes do more for Native American entrepreneurship.

(continued)

Question	Response
Are you a member of business organizations? Are these organizations unique to Native Americans or open to all races? Did they contribute to your business success?	I have been a member of Rotary, Minnesota American Indian Chamber of Commerce, Minneapolis Chamber of Commerce, St. Paul Chamber of Commerce. These organizations are unique to Native American and are open to all races. Yes, they all contributed to my business success as well as mine.
Do you think social networks and personal connections are important to business? Did you use networking when building your business, and are your social networks race based?	Yes, I have used social networks and personal connections to help me and my company. Some of my networks are race based.
If you could give advice to young Native American entrepreneurs or other young people thinking about starting a business, what would be the most important consideration and why?	Pick something with little competition, pick something you can sell to the government, become an MBE/DBE/SBE company as soon as you can and take advantage of these benefits.
Have you been involved in socio-civic organizations or philanthropic work? If so, in which organizations, and what role did you play?	Director of AIOIC—Minneapolis Director of MNOIC—Minnesota Director of MN American Indian Chamber of Commerce President of South Minneapolis Rotary Club Leadership Twin Cities—Minneapolis Chamber of Commerce
What do you see happening to your business in the future? Do you have succession plans in place? Do you see your business being run by family members or professional managers, and why?	My radio show is now on over 40 stations, 3 radio networks, planning on growing it to 100 by the end of 2019. No family members will be taking over my businesses.
Where do you see yourself 10 years from now? What do you think is your legacy to the business community?	I see myself on many radio stations, making money from underwriters, and my construction company should be bigger as well, working my government-funded projects. I currently am a small business consultant showing and telling entrepreneurs the ways to do good business. I am the business warrior for our indigenous communities.

Entrepreneur 9: Tribal Affiliation—Seminole

Question	Response
Kindly provide an overview of your family history. For example, was there an entrepreneur in your family? Did your family history influence your decision to start a business?	My father worked for the Dep't of Interior/Fish and Wildlife for 35 years, and my mother was a stay-at-home mom. Yes, they were entrepreneurs as well; they made men's fancy war dance bustles and bead work.
What was your educational background? Do you have specific views on formal versus informal education? What are your views on Native American entrepreneurial training programs? Has education contributed to your business success?	As soon as I graduated from high school I went straight to college that summer and graduated with a BA in three years. I will always advocate formal education; however, I do understand that it is not for everyone. There should be some type of Native American entrepreneurial training!
Everyone has at least one role model, someone they aspire to be like. Do you have one who is an entrepreneur? How did the role model(s) influence your decision to start a business?	My role model was my father. As I stated above I considered him an entrepreneur with his side hustle of making war dance bustles.
Starting a new business is not an easy process. What motivated you to start one? What steps did you take to start the business?	Currently not a business owner.
What challenges did you face when building your business, and how did you overcome them? Did you come across any unique circumstances as a result of your race?	With my father's little business his customers were all native.

(continued)

Question	Response
What types of support were most helpful to you when you were building your business? For example, did your local community play a role in shaping your business interests and development, or maybe it was a mentor? What or who was the one thing that made you believe, "Yes, I can do this!"	I would have to say doing a market analysis is the very first steps in building an NA-owned business. Research the industry and what would be the industry description and outlook. Taking steps to obtain information about my target market, distinguishing characteristics, size of the primary target market, how much market share could I gain, and what the pricing and gross margin targets are.
What do you think are the essential skills needed for Native American entrepreneurs to succeed in America? Also, what personal attitudes do you think are essential?	Native American entrepreneurs really should have the characteristics and skills commonly associated with successful entrepreneurs, such as comfortable with taking risks, being independent, persuasive, able to negotiate, have creativity, and is supported by others.
If you had the chance to start over again, would you do anything differently? If so, what's the reason?	
How would you characterize the state of Native American entrepreneurship in the United States? For instance, is it in the early stages, is it growing, or is it mature? Do you think it is open to all, or limited to certain individuals? Is it viable from anywhere in the country, or more favorable in certain states?	It is gaining momentum but not at a rate that other races have. More training and opportunities would certainly help. Many do not write or have business plans.
Are you a member of business organizations? Are these organizations unique to Native Americans or open to all races? Did they contribute to your business success?	Formerly worked with National Center for American Indian Enterprise Development, but quite honestly I don't believe their outreach and assistance has helped NA small business owners.
Do you think social networks and personal connections are important to business? Did you use networking when building your business, and are your social networks race based?	

If you could give advice to young Native American entrepreneurs or other young people thinking about starting a business, what would be the most important consideration and why?

WRITE A BUSINESS PLAN!! Ask yourself these 20 questions that they need to think about to begin their preparation and planning of starting a business:

1. Why am I starting a business?
2. What kind of business do I want?
3. Who is my ideal customer?
4. What products or services will my business provide?
5. Am I prepared to spend the time and money to get my business started?
6. What differentiates my business idea and the products or services I will provide from others in the market?
7. Where will my business be located?
8. How many employees will I need?
9. How much money do I need to get started?
10. Will I need to get a loan?
11. How soon will it take before my products or services will be available?
12. How long do I have until I start making a profit?
13. Who is my competition?
14. How will I price my product compared to my competition?
15. How will I set up the legal structure?
16. What taxes do I need to pay?
17. What kind of insurance do I need?
18. How will I manage my business?
19. How will I advertise my business?
20. What type of suppliers will I need?

(continued)

Question	Response
Have you been involved in socio-civic organizations or philanthropic work? If so, in which organizations, and what role did you play?	Not recently
What do you see happening to your business in the future? Do you have succession plans in place? Do you see your business being run by family members or professional managers, and why?	Plan! Plan! Plan! Write a business plan! Would love to see more family-owned-and-run businesses of our Indian people!
Where do you see yourself 10 years from now? What do you think is your legacy to the business community?	Retired! But always willing to be a subject matter expert if needed! ☺

Entrepreneur 10: Tribal Affiliation—Chickasaw

Question	Response
Kindly provide an overview of your family history. For example, was there an entrepreneur in your family? Did your family history influence your decision to start a business?	Parents married over 40 years in middle-class urban area. No entrepreneurs. Mom was a pharmaceutical sales rep and dad was a banker. They instilled a work ethic in my brother and I as we started working at a very young age and had to earn items versus being given to us.
What was your educational background? Do you have specific views on formal versus informal education? What are your views on Native American entrepreneurial training programs? Has education contributed to your business success?	BA in business admin from University of Kansas. MBA in finance from Southern Methodist University. Education has contributed, but I put significantly weight on experience. Education breaks ties.
Everyone has at least one role model, someone they aspire to be like. Do you have one who is an entrepreneur? How did the role model(s) influence your decision to start a business?	Fortunately, I have always had a passion to run a business, so I can't think of one person here.

Starting a new business is not an easy process. What motivated you to start one? What steps did you take to start the business?	Health care delivery system and health outcomes in Indian Country are sad. I was tired of sitting on sidelines and wanted to make a difference. Approximately 70 percent of medical decisions are based on the result of a lab test, and there were no native-focused reference laboratories despite approximately 6 million native lives, so building a medical laboratory is where we were going to start. Steps: I had close friends in laboratory space, so I was able to lean on them. Created business plan and legal entity, secured funding, and hired outstanding lab team.
What challenges did you face when building your business, and how did you overcome them? Did you come across any unique circumstances as a result of your race?	Regulatory hurdles, time, and capital. Medical decisions are made off of our lab results, so we spent months conducting studies to ensure protection of the sample and subsequent results. Labs are capital-intensive, so your cash burn rate is fast. Plus, competition tries to keep you down. Contracting with health insurance companies is also a challenge. Half our staff is native, so we understand Indian Country better than our competition and we performed better, which enabled us to grow.
What types of support were most helpful to you when you were building your business? For example, did your local community play a role in shaping your business interests and development, or maybe it was a mentor? What or who was the one thing that made you believe, "Yes, I can do this!"	Having investors that had built labs, my experience, and our focus on Indian Country gave us confidence we would make it. Hiring top talent in Indian Country definitely helped as well as engaging with the American Indian Chamber of Commerce here in Oklahoma.
What do you think are the essential skills needed for Native American entrepreneurs to succeed in America? Also, what personal attitudes do you think are essential?	Perseverance, ability to raise capital, ability to lead, ability to sell, character, understanding of financials, treat people well.
If you had the chance to start over again, would you do anything differently? If so, what's the reason?	Absolutely, as an entrepreneur I make mistakes every day. You find a way to learn from it and don't make the same ones again.

(continued)

Question	Response
How would you characterize the state of Native American entrepreneurship in the United States? For instance, is it in the early stages, is it growing, or is it mature? Do you think it is open to all, or limited to certain individuals? Is it viable from anywhere in the country, or more favorable in certain states?	I like the future. We have a resiliency and knowledge in our elders with a very energetic youth. I think we are getting better at crossing over tribal boundaries to create more economic development opportunities. We have favorable laws too. We are getting better together as a tribal community and sharing of ideas. We could be better at supporting tribal business, and we are still tentative in areas to takes risks. I have been told that even though there is an opportunity to improve a problem, it is easier to continue blaming someone else versus doing it ourselves. Economic development is definitely different depending on the tribe and state. I am also starting to see tribes diversifying their economic development interests in industries outside of gaming, which is smart and needed.
Are you a member of business organizations? Are these organizations unique to Native Americans or open to all races? Did they contribute to your business success?	American Indian Chamber of Commerce. They have been great.
Do you think social networks and personal connections are important to business? Did you use networking when building your business, and are your social networks race based?	Yes, I am a big social media fan, and they aren't race based, but our connections are native focused.
If you could give advice to young Native American entrepreneurs or other young people thinking about starting a business, what would be the most important consideration and why?	Get experience, be patient, always be learning, and perform. The world is competitive and you need to be able to separate yourself from others. Be willing to do those things that others don't like to do.
Have you been involved in socio-civic organizations or philanthropic work? If so, in which organizations, and what role did you play?	Yes. Church. We sponsor many native entities and focus on giving time and money back into the community. We are an Indian-preferred business in that we like to engage other tribal businesses to help the community.

Question	Response
What do you see happening to your business in the future? Do you have succession plans in place? Do you see your business being run by family members or professional managers, and why?	Depends on the day! ☺ We want to continue to grow geographically and by expanding our product offering. We have a lot to do to help improve health outcomes. My kids are young, so I see my business being run by professional managers someday.
Where do you see yourself 10 years from now? What do you think is your legacy to the business community?	Running Tribal Diagnostics! I hope our legacy is that Tribal Diagnostics helped make a difference in Indian Country health care and economic development. We haven't taken a dime of federal dollars to build and operate the business, and we want to be able to teach tribes to do the same. The answer to help improve health care is at the community level.

Entrepreneur 11: Tribal Affiliation—Caddo of Oklahoma

Question	Response
Kindly provide an overview of your family history. For example, was there an entrepreneur in your family? Did your family history influence your decision to start a business?	My mom was a psychiatrist and my father worked in the oil industry. I had mentors that influenced my decision to go into business.
What was your educational background? Do you have specific views on formal versus informal education? What are your views on Native American entrepreneurial training programs? Has education contributed to your business success?	I have a degree in television and film production. In my case, my degree was helpful but not a necessity.
Everyone has at least one role model, someone they aspire to be like. Do you have one who is an entrepreneur? How did the role model(s) influence your decision to start a business?	Mine was my mother. She gave me the confidence to achieve whatever I set my mind to.

(continued)

Question	Response
Starting a new business is not an easy process. What motivated you to start one? What steps did you take to start the business?	I had things I wanted to say; a lot of research and talking to other entrepreneurs.
What challenges did you face when building your business, and how did you overcome them? Did you come across any unique circumstances as a result of your race?	Financing has always been my biggest obstacle.
What types of support were most helpful to you when you were building your business? For example, did your local community play a role in shaping your business interests and development, or maybe it was a mentor? What or who was the one thing that made you believe, "Yes, I can do this!"	My industry network was my biggest asset.
What do you think are the essential skills needed for Native American entrepreneurs to succeed in America? Also, what personal attitudes do you think are essential?	A strong positive attitude is essential, along with strong community support.
If you had the chance to start over again, would you do anything differently? If so, what's the reason?	I would start smaller and build an audience.
How would you characterize the state of Native American entrepreneurship in the United States? For instance, is it in the early stages, is it growing, or is it mature? Do you think it is open to all, or limited to certain individuals? Is it viable from anywhere in the country, or more favorable in certain states?	I believe it the tip of the iceberg of what we are capable of.
Are you a member of business organizations? Are these organizations unique to Native Americans or open to all races? Did they contribute to your business success?	I'm on LinkedIn. It's open to all and it's a great platform.
Do you think social networks and personal connections are important to business? Did you use networking when building your business, and are your social networks race based?	Not race based. I think social networking is essential for business success.

If you could give advice to young Native American entrepreneurs or other young people thinking about starting a business, what would be the most important consideration and why?	Listen more than you speak and ask good questions.
Have you been involved in socio-civic organizations or philanthropic work? If so, in which organizations, and what role did you play?	I have always tried to give back to my community.
What do you see happening to your business in the future? Do you have succession plans in place? Do you see your business being run by family members or professional managers, and why?	I see my business doing great things.
Where do you see yourself 10 years from now? What do you think is your legacy to the business community?	I would hope to be in a position to give other Native Americans opportunities in business.

Entrepreneur 12: Tribal Affiliation—Quechan

Question	Response
Kindly provide an overview of your family history. For example, was there an entrepreneur in your family? Did your family history influence your decision to start a business?	Many of my family history consists of politicians and traditionalists. Many of which have served our tribe as council men and women, as well as serving in administrative capacities for the tribal government. There were no entrepreneurs in my family, to my knowledge however, each person attempted to identify a need and find a solution. Given that I am also identifying the need to employ tribal members through my organization, I am also attempting to provide a solution to this issue.

(continued)

Question	Response
What was your educational background? Do you have specific views on formal versus informal education? What are your views on Native American entrepreneurial training programs? Has education contributed to your business success?	I currently have degrees in film and video production, business communications, and Indigenous Peoples Law. I believe that there is value in formal and informal training—especially in the age of technology! I believe a mentor is just as valuable as a degree program, given that people are prone to learning in different ways. I believe that Native American entrepreneurial programs are very important to creating sustainability in tribal economies. If we empower more of our people with the knowledge to create and run a business, we will rely less on government funding and eventually become truly sovereign. I believe that formal and informal education has created an opportunity to look through various lenses at how to go about launching a business and managing different aspects of it.
Everyone has at least one role model, someone they aspire to be like. Do you have one who is an entrepreneur? How did the role model(s) influence your decision to start a business?	My entrepreneurial role model is [Name], owner of Poston and Associates, a New Mexico-based communications firm, run by mostly indigenous professionals. I already launched my organization but was in a position where we were needing growth. [Name] became a mentor and role model because she took the time to sow into me the pertinent information I needed to continue leading my organization. She gives me confidence, motivation, and something to aspire to.
Starting a new business is not an easy process. What motivated you to start one? What steps did you take to start the business?	I co-founded my organization because our tribe was a news desert and in need of a resource. We also recognized that our traditional method of face-to-face communication was fading, and we wanted to leverage digital technology to bridge the gap. We found a fiscal sponsor, Ah-Mut Pipa Foundation, and they showed us the ropes on what we needed to do to create the foundations of our business. We came up with a vision and mission, we created an organizational structure, applied for business permits, and also applied for and received our 501 (c) 3 nonprofit status.

What challenges did you face when building your business, and how did you overcome them? Did you come across any unique circumstances as a result of your race?	Raising capital was the hardest challenge we faced as a result of the fact that we didn't have the resources that others may have to fund our business. Marginalized communities usually have less access to funding based on a myriad of factors, including creditworthiness, employment history, savings, etc. This may or may not be a race factor, but statistical evidence proves that tribal reservations face poverty in much higher concentrations than any other minority group.
What types of support were most helpful to you when you were building your business? For example, did your local community play a role in shaping your business interests and development, or maybe it was a mentor? What or who was the one thing that made you believe, "Yes, I can do this!"	All of our efforts were grassroots and we relied solely on engaging our community. Most of the fundraising occurred within our tribal community and that showed us that we could be successful with our organization.
What do you think are the essential skills needed for Native American entrepreneurs to succeed in America? Also, what personal attitudes do you think are essential?	Business acumen, an understanding of basic finances, marketing, and the research skills are necessary to succeed in America. You must know your industry and competition so that you are consistently evolving. I also believe that a positive attitude and emotional intelligence are important personal attitudes to have so that you can pitch your business and generate interest from others.
If you had the chance to start over again, would you do anything differently? If so, what's the reason?	If I could start over again, I would ensure that we put a particular spotlight on creating a strong financial foundation meaning, having our basic business financial documents established early on by a professional.
How would you characterize the state of Native American entrepreneurship in the United States? For instance, is it in the early stages, is it growing, or is it mature? Do you think it is open to all, or limited to certain individuals? Is it viable from anywhere in the country, or more favorable in certain states?	Native American entrepreneurship is blossoming in the United States. With the rise of social media, more entrepreneurs have access to a broader audience and influencers that can motivate anyone to start a business. Still, this may only be open to certain individuals who do not have a knowledge gap in marketing themselves and their brand. This is also true for accessing capital. Many entrepreneurs still need seed money and still face issues in accessing enough to sustain. The barrier for leveraging new media is that some Native American community locations are still so rural that Internet is limited. Cities closer to metro areas most likely experience more exposure and success.

(continued)

Question	Response
Are you a member of business organizations? Are these organizations unique to Native Americans or open to all races? Did they contribute to your business success?	I am a proud member of the Native American Journalism Association, and this type of organization has different sectors that cater to a multitude of races. I only recently joined, but one thing I was able to leverage from my membership was exposure to an application to a workshop for journalists for people of color. I was accepted and was able to create a better pitch deck and a continuity plan for my business.
Do you think social networks and personal connections are important to business? Did you use networking when building your business, and are your social networks race based?	Networking, in general, is important to business whether it is online or in person. You never know what you may learn or what opportunities you may garner from your circle of friends. I leverage native-based and non-native-based networking circles to build my business.
If you could give advice to young Native American entrepreneurs or other young people thinking about starting a business, what would be the most important consideration and why?	The most important piece of advice I would give is that, what you do today will set you up for success tomorrow. Meaning, do something small every day to reach your goal. This means that you have to know your goal, map it out, and figure out what you need to do to get there.
Have you been involved in socio-civic organizations or philanthropic work? If so, in which organizations, and what role did you play?	My organization is a nonprofit organization that is based on serving our community and calling attention to the most pressing topics locally and in Indian Country. We serve the people and that is our main focus, and we do so by designing events, publications, and efforts with the people in mind. I also volunteer 400+ hours per year at schools, churches, and in the community where I live, to ensure that everyone around me is getting a hand when they need it.
What do you see happening to your business in the future? Do you have succession plans in place? Do you see your business being run by family members or professional managers, and why?	I see my organization growing into a full-service media organization that employs tribal members in an onsite and remote environment. I see us contributing to the narrative of native people in America and hosting local and national events to further support and bring attention to our most pressing issues. I would love to create an internship program so that budding journalists, visual communicators, and event organizers a space to start their journey and, eventually, run the organization themselves.

Question	Response
Where do you see yourself 10 years from now? What do you think is your legacy to the business community?	I see myself planting the seed now, in small ways, that will eventually make a big impact in my tribal community, as well as in Indian Country. My legacy would be creating a program as a catalyst for promoting owning our own narrative in America and beyond. This means changing the way our history is portrayed in the media, in schools, and make policy changes that create opportunity for us to truly become sovereign.

Entrepreneur 13: Tribal Affiliation—Quechan

Question	Response
Kindly provide an overview of your family history. For example, was there an entrepreneur in your family? Did your family history influence your decision to start a business?	I was raised by highly successful entrepreneurs. In my younger years, my family practiced beading with the goal of starting a business. My father now owns a corporation and my mother owns a counseling practice. I was raised with the belief that you should never do anything you're good at for free.
What was your educational background? Do you have specific views on formal versus informal education? What are your views on Native American entrepreneurial training programs? Has education contributed to your business success?	I am currently a senior in college as well as a first-year graduate student at GMU. While I've never compared forms of education, I believe that both formal and informal education are important for well-rounded development. I have never participated in a Native American entrepreneurial training program, but I imagine they benefit native students by creating a comfortable environment to learn in. I would like to participate in a Native American training program during my time in graduate school. Lastly, I believe my education has made me more confident in my business endeavors. I'm more comfortable doing research, communicating with others, and applying my skills.

(continued)

Question	Response
Everyone has at least one role model, someone they aspire to be like. Do you have one who is an entrepreneur? How did the role model(s) influence your decision to start a business?	I aspire to be like both of my parents. They are both entrepreneurs that work to improve the success and well-being of other people. My perspective of business stemmed from my parents, who focus on their impact rather than a profit. Their passion, honesty, and openness to change makes them incredibly successful business owners. Their love for their work creates trust among their clients/customers and, in turn, fuels their profits. I've always pictured myself owning a business that is successful simply because I love it and work hard to make an impact.
Starting a new business is not an easy process. What motivated you to start one? What steps did you take to start the business?	I was motivated to start my first business by the size of the market and funding for my graduate degree. I crocheted clothing for women to sell on Etsy. To start, I researched the market, sketched designs, and created prototypes. I also calculated the price of the materials and labor required to make each one for proper pricing. Then I photographed my work and published them on Etsy.
What challenges did you face when building your business, and how did you overcome them? Did you come across any unique circumstances as a result of your race?	I knew I needed to advertise for my creations, but I was scared of the demand that would result. I also feared that my clothing would not fit everyone, leading to difficult conversations with customers and creating new prototypes with skills I wasn't sure I quite had. I never overcame these fears and removed my listings from Etsy. I didn't believe I had enough time to keep up with the work involved with selling my items. I'm unsure if this self-doubt was related to my race, but I struggled with the decision to include my race in the marketing process. I want to create native products for native people one day, but that would involve publicly claiming my identity which I've never felt comfortable doing. I also don't want other people to think I'm attempting to profit off of my race, since I've been told by my peers that I'm not actually "Native American."

What types of support were most helpful to you when you were building your business? For example, did your local community play a role in shaping your business interests and development, or maybe it was a mentor? What or who was the one thing that made you believe, "Yes, I can do this!"	I benefitted most from personal support from friends and family. I struggled with doubting my abilities, and the praise I received from my loved ones helped me feel more confident in myself. My mother and father contributed the most to this confidence; however, I never regained the motivation to try again.
What do you think are the essential skills needed for Native American entrepreneurs to succeed in America? Also, what personal attitudes do you think are essential?	I believe Native American entrepreneurs need social support and confidence to succeed. Hundreds of years were dedicated to silencing indigenous people, and I believe this has greatly affected the way natives see themselves and their futures.
If you had the chance to start over again, would you do anything differently? If so, what's the reason?	While selling handmade items is just the beginning of my business endeavors, I believe there are many other options I have for products to sell. If I could start over, I would practice on my skills more before starting to sell.
How would you characterize the state of Native American entrepreneurship in the United States? For instance, is it in the early stages, is it growing, or is it mature? Do you think it is open to all, or limited to certain individuals? Is it viable from anywhere in the country, or more favorable in certain states?	I believe Native American entrepreneurship is growing as more natives become educated.
Are you a member of business organizations? Are these organizations unique to Native Americans or open to all races? Did they contribute to your business success?	I am not currently a member of any business organization.
Do you think social networks and personal connections are important to business? Did you use networking when building your business, and are your social networks race based?	I believe both social networks and personal connections are vital to a successful business. I did not use networking in my business because I was too afraid of the demand it might cause.
If you could give advice to young Native American entrepreneurs or other young people thinking about starting a business, what would be the most important consideration and why?	I would advise young people to choose a business in which they feel confident pursuing. It's important to stick with something, despite the setbacks one may encounter.

(continued)

Question	Response
Have you been involved in socio-civic organizations or philanthropic work? If so, in which organizations, and what role did you play?	I am currently the president of GMU's Eta Sigma Gamma chapter, a national public health honor society. We aim to improve the health of our community through peer education, volunteering, and fundraising.
What do you see happening to your business in the future? Do you have succession plans in place? Do you see your business being run by family members or professional managers, and why?	I want to restart my shop soon, but I plan to approach it with more confidence. I aim to perfect my products and add a donation component to each sale to help people in need. This way I could bring in extra income to support myself through grad school as well as help people who may need warm, handmade clothing. During my time in graduate school, I will begin planning how I can apply my degree to create a business within the public health sector.
Where do you see yourself 10 years from now? What do you think is your legacy to the business community?	In 10 years, I believe I will be working in epidemiology for a local or state government. I would love to work with Indian Health Service to improve the lives of native people. I don't believe I have formed a legacy yet, but I plan to make a large impact—once I figure out how!

Entrepreneur 14: Tribal Affiliation—Oglala Sioux

Question	Response
Kindly provide an overview of your family history. For example, was there an entrepreneur in your family? Did your family history influence your decision to start a business?	My family is all from the reservation and is from generations of survival and reservation and economic poverty. The closest thing to entrepreneurship is selling of art, but not official business. My grandma makes star quilts and sews beautiful pillows and other items to supplement her social security. This is how she has survived her entire life, on her art. My mother does quilting for people who need a star quilt put together and they have the tops. This is her income. I decided to start business after learning skills in my MBA program. The influence my family had on my business was the content of my art and the idea that I must break the poverty cycle, and have some fun while doing it.

What was your educational background? Do you have specific views on formal versus informal education? What are your views on Native American entrepreneurial training programs? Has education contributed to your business success?	I have formal education, with a bachelor of arts in psychology at UCLA, as well as an MBA from a private East Coast School. I spent 10 years working in native nonprofit and higher ed. work. I think native entrepreneurial training programs are important because those programs are probably the sole source of business education that many receive if they are not from a wealthy family or a family who has owned business on the reservation from generation to generation. The training opens gates that would otherwise be closed.
Everyone has at least one role model, someone they aspire to be like. Do you have one who is an entrepreneur? How did the role model(s) influence your decision to start a business?	Business wise, my greatest role models are [Name] and [Name]. [Name] had foresight and created a future he wanted. [Name] is an artist that has shops across the world, selling his graphic art work on apparel. I want to be like both of them, having foresight and expanding globally, doing what I love.
Starting a new business is not an easy process. What motivated you to start one? What steps did you take to start the business?	My MBA, as well as attending the American Indigenous Business Leaders (AIBL) conference in 2017 as a business plan competition participant was the turning point. I was thinking about starting a fashion line and did test marketing to raise money for a class trip to Germany. Building a team business plan, taught me first-hand skills on all the aspects that entail creating a business as well as walking away with a viable finished product. While at AIBL, I went to the session on how to create e-commerce and learned who to set up a shopify shop and use drop shipping. This is a very low-risk strategy as sales and expenses are taken care of in the beginning and you get the difference in your pocket, without worrying about inventory, shipping, etc. Having a full-time job, this was the best approach.

(*continued*)

Question	Response
What challenges did you face when building your business, and how did you overcome them? Did you come across any unique circumstances as a result of your race?	The biggest challenges I have in building and expanding my business is marketing and social media expansion. I've been building networks in the local arena; however, nationally, a majority of my customers are friends that I've personally made in my life and travels. Getting help from people who are in higher positions as mentors was very hard for me. These people who I looked to for support were fellow natives and not feeling camaraderie from those who are super successful was challenging. I've learned to stick to only people who have been supportive in the beginning and who are supportive now. My race was not a challenge, other than quite successful natives would not help me, probably because I am native too.
What types of support were most helpful to you when you were building your business? For example, did your local community play a role in shaping your business interests and development, or maybe it was a mentor? What or who was the one thing that made you believe, "Yes, I can do this!"	I think the greatest support was and is friends buying from my business and helping promote. I asked for a lot of photos to help keep my social media content going. I met a lot of local artists who are very supportive and authentic. We buy from each other and are a positive energy. I recently moved into an art studio because of the local network. A local fashion designer invited me to participate in the Native POP fashion show, which led to exposure, and I was invited again a year later. Seeing people locally who know who I am as a designer, and buying my apparel, especially if I don't know them personally, makes me feel good. They like my work. At the end of the day, I do the business for the enjoyment and for the artistic fulfillment. Money is not the driving force so I don't feel stressed about making money since I have a full-time job that is my primary income.

What do you think are the essential skills needed for Native American entrepreneurs to succeed in America? Also, what personal attitudes do you think are essential?	Grit, resilience, putting in hard work, understanding how to minimize costs and maximize profits, knowing that you can't do it alone, networking capabilities, and understanding that everyone you meet is a potential customer and to treat them with the best customer service you can give. Be generous and don't have a Western mindset about business, because it's up to us to change the perspective. Every native entrepreneur and professional is a part of a movement to change the United States and the world.
If you had the chance to start over again, would you do anything differently? If so, what's the reason?	I think I would have taken the time to have better planning. The reason is mainly marketing and having a solid marketing campaign. Thinking before acting, and planning in advance would have kept me organized because family, unexpected events work take up a lot of my time and my business has been put on the back burners.
How would you characterize the state of Native American entrepreneurship in the United States? For instance, is it in the early stages, is it growing, or is it mature? Do you think it is open to all, or limited to certain individuals? Is it viable from anywhere in the country, or more favorable in certain states?	There is a database of native business owners, and I believe it is 100s. It's growing and the potential is in the urban areas on the West and East Coast, as well as online. Online opens up to a global market. Individuals with the knowledge or experience, and ability to secure huge capital are the ones who have larger businesses. Those who do not have that access, like myself, are not able to grow as fast. Also, entrepreneurs who can dedicate their full time to their business is key. I don't have the ability to not work, because profits will not cover my expenses and I support more than just myself. Those who already have the ability to live even when their business is not making profits is a very privileged sect of Native Americans.
Are you a member of business organizations? Are these organizations unique to Native Americans or open to all races? Did they contribute to your business success?	I am an alumnus of AIBL. AIBL is amazing and has been immensely supportive. AIBL commissioned me for a t-shirt design for their conference last year, and they were happy with the end product.

(continued)

Question	Response
Do you think social networks and personal connections are important to business? Did you use networking when building your business, and are your social networks race based?	Social networks and personal connections are key. They are your most loyal fans. I used networking to build my business, especially in the branding and marketing materials. Quite a bit in my network are Native Americans; however, my target market is nonnatives.
If you could give advice to young Native American entrepreneurs or other young people thinking about starting a business, what would be the most important consideration and why?	Having a plan and utilizing your free and personal resources. SBA, Local Native Community Development Financial Institutions, anyone who is willing to mentor you and give you advice. There will be many who will discourage you and others who will encourage you and give you tidbits of advance. For every rejection I get from individuals, I find someone who has good things to say like [Name] and [Name], high-profile native fashion designers who gave me encouragement and tidbits of advice. I don't see my business being run my anyone but myself because it's one of the few aspects I can control in life. I love management. I think that eventually I'd like to hire a social media marketer to help bring more buzz and movement to my brand.
Have you been involved in socio-civic organizations or philanthropic work? If so, in which organizations, and what role did you play?	I've worked at UCLA in student-run, student-led native support initiatives as coordinators when I was a student and director of a program after graduation. I've worked at my local tribal college as a student support counselor. I've worked in partnership with Native Americans as a collaboration and training specialist, and I currently work at First Peoples Fund as a program manager of community development. Throughout my life time, I've volunteered to support the native community, particularly in Los Angeles and raised money for a youth journey. I also started and left a project in Boston, that brought Lakota youth to Boston once a year. It became successful; however, I had to leave due to conflicts in ideologies from the nonnatives who used my expertise but did not see me as equal in the decision-making. She was not working in the best interest of the community and approached the project in a way of self-glorification and white-saviorism. I will not work with that again ever in my life.

Question	Response
What do you see happening to your business in the future? Do you have succession plans in place? Do you see your business being run by family members or professional managers, and why?	I see this business in particular to be more of a hobby than a full-fledged business. I only see hiring a social media marketer to help with keeping active and creating buzz online. I'm actually interested in testing a start-up or two in collaboration with investors and getting a loan. These are things I actually want to pursue on a more formal level.
Where do you see yourself 10 years from now? What do you think is your legacy to the business community?	I am hoping 10 years from now I am in retirement or in a good place to retire early. I am hoping that my businesses have been successful and I am able to hire and train young native people to development into professionals that can rise to upper-level management not just in my business but any business. I want our native youth to be better professionals than anyone else, create financial wealth for themselves and their families, and have fun, travel, and see life as an adventure rather than a struggle.

Entrepreneur 15: Tribal Affiliation—Diné (Navajo)

Question	Response
Kindly provide an overview of your family history. For example, was there an entrepreneur in your family? Did your family history influence your decision to start a business?	I am the little Diné (Navajo) girl who attended Bureau of Indian Affairs boarding schools where I dealt with confusion between the culture I love and a different culture that was presented. While attending public schools, my day started at 4:30 a.m. when I woke up to catch the bus to school 40 miles away. My upbringing was shaped by my late grandfather and father who led our family like our Diné (Navajo) Chief Manuelito did by leading our people during and after the Long Walk Period. I've heard stories about Chief Manuelito, and it's no wonder our elders were such great leaders around our communities.

(continued)

Question	Response
	Just as equally important and inspirational, womenfolk did their part in our upbringing, keeping the home fires going. Our hard-working grandparents and parents were known for their craft skills with men making silver with turquoise jewelry and women weaving Navajo rugs to sell or trade. As a little girl I've seen my mother sell her rugs to the local trading post owner in Cowsprings, AZ and sold rugs to professors during my higher education days in Phoenix, AZ. I have to wonder if I got my entrepreneurial blood from my mother. Having been raised in one of the most remote areas in Arizona, life was hard, as we were poor. Nonetheless, growing up with hard-working family and my grandfather telling me "never turn your back on your own people" is what I believe led me to start on the entrepreneurial path.
What was your educational background? Do you have specific views on formal versus informal education? What are your views on Native American entrepreneurial training programs? Has education contributed to your business success?	I graduated from Tuba City High School in Tuba City, AZ on Navajo Reservation and went on to higher education where I graduated with my Bachelor of Science in Computer Information Systems from Arizona State University. I'm a firm believer of a balanced learning environment between formal and informal education. An example is college/university students taken out of their class sessions and allowed to volunteer at economic development–focused conferences. In exchange for their volunteer services, they are allowed to participate in workshops with various topics and networking sessions. This way they see live workforce in action where private companies of all sizes, and federal/state/local organizations come together and network. I cannot stress enough to get the students out of the educational classroom bubble while they're still in college/universities. My views on Native American entrepreneurial training programs, based on my experience with SBA's e200 Emerging Leaders initiative with a focus on Native American business owners' seven-month training, was given in a Western non-indigenous orientation.

	As indigenous entrepreneurs, we need Native American entrepreneurial training programs inclusive of both nonindigenous and indigenous holistic attitudes. Yes, I believe my CIS studies at ASU contributed to my business but is a complement to experience and planning making all critical factors playing a role in working toward business success.
Everyone has at least one role model, someone they aspire to be like. Do you have one who is an entrepreneur? How did the role model(s) influence your decision to start a business?	A former employer played a pivotal role in helping me start on the entrepreneurial path. This small business owner allowed me to shadow her while she networked outside of my office. She provided me the tools with resources and allowed me to get from Point A to Point B without micromanaging me. I grew professionally from this experience as a program manager. End of 2011, she tells me, "if you can do all this, why not do it for yourself (your own company)?" This type of encouragement was influential in starting my own business.
Starting a new business is not an easy process. What motivated you to start one? What steps did you take to start the business?	First, I love working with computers, so I built my passion to work in information system industry. Secondly, having been a W-2 employee for both public and private organization, I experienced the greatest satisfaction, and the sense of pride I feel is when giving service back to my own tribesmen. I'm thinking this pride stems back to my grandfather telling me not to turn my back on my own people. I also realized if working as a W-2 employee for another company, you would always have to do what company owner wants you to do. If you're working for a nonnative business and if a Native American client comes along, you wouldn't be able to deliver services tailored to the indigenous needs as the nonnative business wouldn't know how. When I started my business, aside from registering my business with the state and getting EIN, I started taking SBA's small business workshops in person in addition to doing some webinars.

(continued)

Question	Response
What challenges did you face when building your business, and how did you overcome them? Did you come across any unique circumstances as a result of your race?	As a very shy Diné woman, it was hard for me to communicate. This challenge was hard to overcome since we were brought up where eye contact was avoided and being told "talk only when necessary." Knowing that by being in business, you are always in a position where you need to "sell" not only with communication skill, but also with persuading people to buy your offerings. So, I started volunteering at major conferences to learn how to network and getting in front of buyers. There was a bit of challenge to gain credibility from my tribal community where computer services providers are normally male business owners, but once I obtained tribal preference contracting certification, I was able to get past the obstacle.
What types of support were most helpful to you when you were building your business? For example, did your local community play a role in shaping your business interests and development, or maybe it was a mentor? What or who was the one thing that made you believe, "Yes, I can do this!"	I joined Meet-Up and started attending Women Who Code group meetings where people talked about the latest in content management systems with website development. Women Who Code group meetings are also a good source of "Yes, I can do this!" motivation for me.
What do you think are the essential skills needed for Native American entrepreneurs to succeed in America? Also, what personal attitudes do you think are essential?	Professionally, communication and a go-getter attitude are definitely needed to succeed. At the personal level, self-discipline that encompasses honesty, responsibility, and accountability intertwined with cultural values are all essential. As for my business, marketing as culturally competent and being fluent in my Native American (Diné) language has helped me with some contracting opportunities.
If you had the chance to start over again, would you do anything differently? If so, what's the reason?	Spend more time studying financial literacy early on to know my business health using financial ratios at any point and given time. This is important to me because, I don't want to be operating blindly and knowing financial ratios will help me make informed business decision.

How would you characterize the state of Native American entrepreneurship in the United States? For instance, is it in the early stages, is it growing, or is it mature? Do you think it is open to all, or limited to certain individuals? Is it viable from anywhere in the country, or more favorable in certain states?	Maybe it just feels that way because I'm a Native American entrepreneur, but I think it is in a growing stage with an exciting and attractive growth rate. Entrepreneurship is for anyone who is willing to work hard for to build the passion they have for service/product they decide to sell and who is a risk-taker knowing there is no guarantee for success, all while maintaining balance between business and family. Now with technology advancements putting information at our fingertips, entrepreneurship can be done from anywhere in the country where there is Internet available. On the other hand, Native American entrepreneurship from rural reservations in Arizona still has intermittent Internet connections, which make it challenging to run a business.
Are you a member of business organizations? Are these organizations unique to Native Americans or open to all races? Did they contribute to your business success?	I belong to a group called Native Women Entrepreneurs of Arizona (NWEAZ) where Native American women–owned business owners meet every other month to discuss obstacles and empower one another. NWEAZ is open to Native American women–owned businesses only. Yes, within a year of joining the group, I not only learned how to overcome some obstacles but also gained two clients from NWEAZ group networking sessions.
Do you think social networks and personal connections are important to business? Did you use networking when building your business, and are your social networks race based?	Knowing digital presence with social networks is no longer an option; I use both physical and digital marketing when building my business. Social networks and personal connections are a must when running a business, so I plan to invest in an improved business social media platform. My business social networks and digital presence is not entirely race based, but some of the services offered indicate cultural competency leading to a message that might be saying our niche is Native America, which I am okay with.

(continued)

Question	Response
If you could give advice to young Native American entrepreneurs or other young people thinking about starting a business, what would be the most important consideration and why?	To the young Native American people in general, they should be encouraged as much as possible about how they need to be "coachable" in life. Develop a blue print of what you envision your business goal(s) to be using a business plan. Follow that blue print as a road map with perseverance, but with a continual review of your goals and change them as you grow your business.
Have you been involved in socio-civic organizations or philanthropic work? If so, in which organizations, and what role did you play?	For years I volunteered at the National Center for American Indian Enterprise Development NCAIED's Reservation Economic Summit (RES) in Las Vegas helping with event planning with attendee registration support services focus and as the lead volunteer coordinator until 2015 when my business was hired as the lead event registration consultant. In August 2018, I donated a website to Native Women Entrepreneurs of Arizona using a subdomain of my business website hosting service plan, and I am currently the website manager donating my time.
What do you see happening to your business in the future? Do you have succession plans in place? Do you see your business being run by family members or professional managers, and why?	While my business is still in the first stage of business growth (existence), I see my business having the solid professional management team to help me run the business. I am currently in the process of forming a team of subject matter experts as resource to hire, but I don't have a clear succession plan in place yet. I don't see my business run by family members, because my immediate family members all have a different career path.
Where do you see yourself 10 years from now? What do you think is your legacy to the business community?	I see my business as a top leader in automation of knowledge work in Indian Country as well as being one of the major big data contributors to tribal nations to use for economic develop on Indian Reservations, which are low-income, developing nations.

Entrepreneur 16: Tribal Affiliation—Quechan

Question	Response
Kindly provide an overview of your family history. For example, was there an entrepreneur in your family? Did your family history influence your decision to start a business?	I'm an enrolled member of the Quechan Nation. My parents were "entrepreneurs" you could say. Although, at the time I don't think it was referred to as being an entrepreneur. They sold jewelry and crafts at pow-wows and gatherings. We would travel with them all the time. It was like a second income for them. After a while, my brother and me would start selling things too. My brother would sell badges, and I would sell bumper stickers. Since my parents didn't have a lot of money, this is how we would raise money to buy things we wanted. Sometimes we would make gourd rattles and sell them too. We would also collect cans and bottles to raise money. After my parents divorced, I got a paper route to raise money to help me buy school clothes. We would also put ads in the newspaper classifieds to mow lawns or pull weeds. I never thought of it as being an entrepreneur. It was what we had to do. But it did play a major role in my decisions later in life. I don't think I ever consciously thought that it had an influence on me starting my business. I was just brought up knowing that if you wanted something you had to go out and earn it yourself. It was just something you did.

(continued)

Question	Response
What was your educational background? Do you have specific views on formal versus informal education? What are your views on Native American entrepreneurial training programs? Has education contributed to your business success?	My educational background is I have a BA in film production from San Francisco State University. I think both formal and informal education has its benefits. I talk about this when I do presentations about my business and me. My formal education at SFSU was great in providing me with the theories and methods of filmmaking, along with giving me hands-on access to equipment, but it was after graduating that I got real-life experience. Luckily, I found a mentor that took me under his wing and helped me gain work experience in the field. He was an independent filmmaker and had been supporting himself for years. He kind of showed me the ropes. I think entrepreneurial training programs are awesome and needed. California Indian Manpower Consortium has an entrepreneurial training program. They bring me out to be a guest speaker every year. It's amazing to watch the students come alive, especially at the end when they present their business plans. I would recommend that youth be able to take an entrepreneurial training program as well. There's much more creativity involved in starting and maintaining a business than people realize. Many tribal people are already entrepreneurs, and they don't even know it. Taking a class will just help you get organized and become more profitable. Both formal and informal education has contributed to my success.
Everyone has at least one role model, someone they aspire to be like. Do you have one who is an entrepreneur? How did the role model(s) influence your decision to start a business?	I have several role models. I don't think they directly influenced me to start my business. Some have given me skills to have confidence in going out on my own and pursuing my dreams. Others are just super supportive.

Starting a new business is not an easy process. What motivated you to start one? What steps did you take to start the business?	What motivated me to start my own business was the flexibility to work when I wanted. When I moved back to Yuma, AZ, I was very active in language revitalization and cultural learning. Starting my own business gave me the opportunity to do this. Different tribes also contacted me about doing film projects and youth training workshops, so the business kind of created itself. Not until later on did I create the LLC and really push me as a business. It was a very organic process.
What challenges did you face when building your business, and how did you overcome them? Did you come across any unique circumstances as a result of your race?	I think the challenges are ongoing for me. I'm like an independent contractor, so I have to continually be proactive to raise money for projects and seek out film work. I think one of the biggest challenges is building a strong reputation in the native community. I've worked hard to build and maintain my reputations as a creative, hard-working, and dependable filmmaker. I think another major challenge is getting potential clients to see the importance and value film can have in their communities. That the investment outweighs the returns beyond financial.
	I do come across unique circumstances because of my race. I think the main one is trust, especially in the native community. There has been a lot of times that I have been looked over for jobs by larger successful tribes as they tend to get nonnatives to produce work for them. I'm more then capable, but that would rather pick a nonnative company over me. This is frustrating and takes money out of my pocket! If these larger successful tribes would reinvest in our own native professionals, we would all become successful.
What types of support were most helpful to you when you were building your business? For example, did your local community play a role in shaping your business interests and development, or maybe it was a mentor? What or who was the one thing that made you believe, "Yes, I can do this!"	Like I said earlier, I was raised this way. I already knew how to be proactive and seek out work. That's why I think teaching youth about entrepreneurship is important. They can learn early how to make things happen.

(continued)

Question	Response
What do you think are the essential skills needed for Native American entrepreneurs to succeed in America? Also, what personal attitudes do you think are essential?	Essential Skills: Wanting to learn. Being proactive and persistent. Being able to ask for help. Following through when things get tough. Continually educating yourself. Attitudes: The willingness to learn. Willing to admit you don't know something. Be humble and willing to change. Do your best to stay positive when times are tough.
If you had the chance to start over again, would you do anything differently? If so, what's the reason?	Yes, I would be better organized. I wish I knew about and had taken a small business training workshop early on, so I would have a better understanding of all the things you need to do, like taxes and bookkeeping. I would also think about trying to find investors or partners. I think my business has a potential for growth, but I'm learning that this growth can only come through developing partnerships or finding investors. This may be my next step.
How would you characterize the state of Native American entrepreneurship in the United States? For instance, is it in the early stages, is it growing, or is it mature? Do you think it is open to all, or limited to certain individuals? Is it viable from anywhere in the country, or more favorable in certain states?	I think the state of native entrepreneurships in the United States and beyond has yet to be fully tapped. I think natives have always been entrepreneurs. Frybread stands, jewelry and crafts, vending at powwows, is all entrepreneurship to me. But I don't think we have really thought of this as entrepreneurship until recently. I think the potential to create jobs and revenue streams for tribal members is barely getting started. If the more successful tribal gaming enterprises would reinvest in our communities, I think the potential to create more work and employment is limitless. But it's going to take a community effort on a national scale. I also believe the Internet has the potential to bring jobs and revenue to small isolated tribal communities as well.
Are you a member of business organizations? Are these organizations unique to Native Americans or open to all races? Did they contribute to your business success?	I am not, but I think the potential is there if I need it.

Do you think social networks and personal connections are important to business? Did you use networking when building your business, and are your social networks race based?	Yes, yes, and yes.
If you could give advice to young Native American entrepreneurs or other young people thinking about starting a business, what would be the most important consideration and why?	Don't be afraid to ask for help. Find a mentor. If there are classes for small business, then go! Put your business on paper. Write a business plan. Come up with a mission statement and vision. This will help you define what your business is.
Have you been involved in socio-civic organizations or philanthropic work? If so, in which organizations, and what role did you play?	No.
What do you see happening to your business in the future? Do you have succession plans in place? Do you see your business being run by family members or professional managers, and why?	This is a scary question. As I get older, I'm starting to realize the importance of having a retirement plan. This is something that was never taught to me, and I'm learning on my own about this. As a small business owner you need to start setting up your own retirement plan. Unlike working for an employer who helps set up your retirement, you have to do it yourself.
Where do you see yourself 10 years from now? What do you think is your legacy to the business community?	Well, that all depends on if this next film becomes a hit or not. If it does, then I'm retiring early. If it doesn't, looks like I'll continue working. Right now, I'm thinking about going back to school and getting my MFA. I think I would like to teach and share my knowledge about filmmaking and business. Through the 20 years I've been doing this, I think I've gained a lot of knowledge that I could share with people and help them. I hope my legacy will be someday people will look back at the films I made and it will have changed their lives for the better. That if I can get one person to personally invest in learning their language or culture, then I've succeeded!

(continued)

Entrepreneur 17: Tribal Affiliation—Chumash

Question	Response
Kindly provide an overview of your family history. For example, was there an entrepreneur in your family? Did your family history influence your decision to start a business?	I think it did. My dad is Chumash (and we met when I was 25). I had a strong role model in my mother and I tended to follow her lead. I found that my father was an entrepreneur and that focus carried me forward. I've always had strong women in my family and that includes my sister. I didn't really have anyone to set the stage for me as an entrepreneur.
What was your educational background? Do you have specific views on formal versus informal education? What are your views on Native American entrepreneurial training programs? Has education contributed to your business success?	I come from humble means and I tend to be very pragmatic. I have a BA from University of California (UC) Santa Barbara and master's degree. I've learned to embrace the things I'm good at, and the things I'm not good at, like accounting. So, for me, it's critical to have a good accountant near me. I tend not to be the smartest guy in the room; however, I always seek a collective approach to the world. I know you need to listen well and to have strong people around me. I started my business in 2002 and I've spent years fine-tuning.
Everyone has at least one role model, someone they aspire to be like. Do you have one who is an entrepreneur? How did the role model(s) influence your decision to start a business?	I guess my parents, and specifically my dad, were my role models. My mom is go-go-go and my dad has the entrepreneurial spirit and he tends to have a bright outlook on life. If I followed my mom, I'd be a workaholic, and by following my dad I am able to seek balance in my life.
Starting a new business is not an easy process. What motivated you to start one? What steps did you take to start the business?	I was in voiceover IP with WorldCom before that crashed, and I began to learn about the 8a program as a native; so I looked into it and found someone to teach me. I met a Cherokee native that owned a small business, and he took me under his wing. He was about to retire and he told me, "can you choose to learn this or not?" So I chose to learn the business from him, and over time I learned business development, direct labor work, back office, and now to run a business. Over time, I was able to take myself off of direct labor, afford myself off of direct labor. My mentor was a blessing to me in so many ways. He even vouched for my security clearance.

What challenges did you face when building your business, and how did you overcome them? Did you come across any unique circumstances as a result of your race?	Yes, because I learned of my native background at 25 years old, I often wondered why I was the only dark-skinned family member. I learned that I need to overcome challenges in my own way. As a business owner, I learned that cash flow is important and especially invoicing. I wasn't born on the reservation, and I often felt guilty about that, I mean how could I speak to rez kids and adults if I wasn't raised there? 8a is race based, for example, if you are an African American, no one cares where in the country you're born. Natives are very different, and they care very much where you were born. I've tried hard to give back to the community. I was asked by Microsoft to travel to Boston, to give a lecture to the "girls who code" and several other native lectures across the United States.
What types of support were most helpful to you when you were building your business? For example, did your local community play a role in shaping your business interests and development, or maybe it was a mentor? What or who was the one thing that made you believe, "Yes, I can do this?"	Well, my mentor was named [name], and he wasn't born on the rez either. He was a Vietnam Veteran and he really helped me. I followed his lead. He taught me different contracting routes and basically spoon-fed me this information. I understand how rare this is and I try to share information as often as possible on government contracting.
What do you think are the essential skills needed for Native American entrepreneurs to succeed in America? Also, what personal attitudes do you think are essential?	I think it depends on my being native. I grew up in a close-knit but very tough environment. My dad is very active and helps me to "smell the roses." My advice would be to give back, know your roots, don't be a fake, and no matter what, know you are Native American and try to give back. Remember those that helped you and remember that you don't have to feel sorry, lend a hand to those who want it.
If you had the chance to start over again, would you do anything differently? If so, what's the reason?	I would use the nine years given by the SBA differently. I'd try not to bite off more than I could chew, learn quicker to under-promise and over-deliver. The SBA froze my sole sourcing capabilities abruptly and that hurt my business a tad. Back then the SBA made no attempt to help you and you were on your own until they stopped you often quite blindly.

(continued)

Question	Response
How would you characterize the state of Native American entrepreneurship in the United States? For instance, is it in the early stages, is it growing, or is it mature? Do you think it is open to all, or limited to certain individuals? Is it viable from anywhere in the country, or more favorable in certain states?	NA businesses have grown, and government contracting has had a huge revenue boost for tribes everywhere. Some tribes have heavy alcoholism and drug abuse rates, and these kids on those reservations have no idea how to learn business. I made some suggesting's to my alma mater to open government contracting and casino management courses to help tribal communities.
Are you a member of business organizations? Are these organizations unique to Native Americans or open to all races? Did they contribute to your business success?	I am a member of Native American Contracting Association (NACA), and they are unique to native businesses. They have contributed to my business success and worked to harm it at the same time.
Do you think social networks and personal connections are important to business? Did you use networking when building your business, and are your social networks race based?	Social networks are important to native communities. High demand for business development people to critical job roles can be filled by social networks. I do use social networks to help build my business, and when I worked hard as a subcontractor, I saw social networking as a critical element of my success.
If you could give advice to young Native American entrepreneurs or other young people thinking about starting a business, what would be the most important consideration and why?	First let's state that kids should start before high school learning business skills. Natives are recruited heavily by businesses and early knowledge will help them to succeed. I would say find a mentor—maybe right one on your reservation and learn all that I could. Whether art, or building something, Native American leaders are in high demand now to run businesses.
Have you been involved in socio-civic organizations or philanthropic work? If so, in which organizations, and what role did you play?	I am involved with the NACA, and they have a yearly leadership week. Tribes sponsor young people to learn business skills, and I sit on a panel with other native business owners.

Question	Response
What do you see happening to your business in the future? Do you have succession plans in place? Do you see your business being run by family members or professional managers, and why?	I see my children may be taking over the business or selling it one day. I'll likely be involved with the Chumash in California and help them with government contracting. I may sell the business also.
Where do you see yourself 10 years from now? What do you think is your legacy to the business community?	I think my legacy is to help those who don't understand government contracting. I like speaking to people and keep doing what you are doing. I'm still here, still in business, and still in an industry I love.

Entrepreneur 18: Tribal Affiliation—Quechan

Question	Response
Kindly provide an overview of your family history. For example, was there an entrepreneur in your family? Did your family history influence your decision to start a business?	I do not remember an entrepreneur from my family per se. I would not say my family history influenced my decision to start a business. I believe my drive to start a business was instilled by my father and my brother and their work ethic.
What was your educational background? Do you have specific views on formal versus informal education? What are your views on Native American entrepreneurial training programs? Has education contributed to your business success?	I have a bachelors in arts and business management degree. I do not believe a formal education is needed to have a successful business. It takes a lot of hard work and the knowledge to how to make sound business decisions. I do believe my education has made my business more successful. I am not aware of any Native American entrepreneurial training programs.
Everyone has at least one role model, someone they aspire to be like. Do you have one who is an entrepreneur? How did the role model(s) influence your decision to start a business?	My role model is without a doubt my brother. He is the epitome of a successful, educated, and hard-working person. He works harder than any other person I have ever met, beside my father. He is wise beyond his years and always has been since I can remember. His influence has illustrated that you can start a business and no one can tell you otherwise.

(continued)

Question	Response
Starting a new business is not an easy process. What motivated you to start one? What steps did you take to start the business?	Starting a business is not that difficult if you have a plan to do exactly that. Getting to know the business you would like to start is paramount. Having even the smallest bit of knowledge in the business you would like to start cannot be taken lightly. After working in or learning the business you would like to start, the process to begin the business gets a little easier.
What challenges did you face when building your business, and how did you overcome them? Did you come across any unique circumstances as a result of your race?	In building my business, I feel it is the same for most new businesses, "getting the word out." I do not remember any specific incidents where my race caused any unique circumstances.
What types of support were most helpful to you when you were building your business? For example, did your local community play a role in shaping your business interests and development, or maybe it was a mentor? What or who was the one thing that made you believe, "Yes, I can do this!"	The support from local government entities proved invaluable. Also, working in the industry already, it was a little easier to understand just exactly what is needed to start and run a successful business. Getting that first estimate and job completed was a good indicator for me that I could, in fact, "do this on my own."
What do you think are the essential skills needed for Native American entrepreneurs to succeed in America? Also, what personal attitudes do you think are essential?	I believe for Native Americans trying to become entrepreneurs, they need to have the passion that any other business owner has, that is, to be successful. They need to not let relatives and friends take away from what they are trying to accomplish.
If you had the chance to start over again, would you do anything differently? If so, what's the reason?	In my specific case, I am happy where I am with my business and do not know that there is anything I would change.

How would you characterize the state of Native American entrepreneurship in the United States? For instance, is it in the early stages, is it growing, or is it mature? Do you think it is open to all, or limited to certain individuals? Is it viable from anywhere in the country, or more favorable in certain states?	Unfortunately, I am not aware of the state of the Native American entrepreneurship in the United States. I believe it might be difficult for Native Americans that live on, or near, a reservation. I believe the difficulty would be generated by family and friends and the culture atmosphere of a typical reservation.
Are you a member of business organizations? Are these organizations unique to Native America or open to all races? Did they contribute to your business success?	I am not a member currently of any business organizations.
Do you think social networks and personal connections are important to business? Did you use networking when building your business, and are your social networks race based?	My business deals a great deal in networking. They are driven by a specific group of people that can affect my business in a good, or bad, direction.
If you could give advice to young Native American entrepreneurs or other young people thinking about starting a business, what would be the most important consideration and why?	Understand your business and start with a good (realistic) business plan. Business plans give you a great perspective of what to expect.
Have you been involved in socio-civic organizations or philanthropic work? If so, in which organizations, and what role did you play?	I have not been involved with any of the organizations mentioned.
What do you see happening to your business in the future? Do you have succession plans in place? Do you see your business being run by family members or professional managers, and why?	I hope to have my business running well enough that I can put people in place, pay them a great wage, and oversee the operations only. If my business is still in place when my children are old enough to run it, that would be great.
Where do you see yourself 10 years from now? What do you think is your legacy to the business community?	Ten years from now I hope to be retiring from my 9-to-5 job and living comfortably on my small business. I hope to start playing a more active role in putting my company's name in the community and doing what I can to volunteer. I would hope that 10 years from now my business is a staple to my community.

(continued)

Entrepreneur 19: Tribal Affiliation—Yaqui

Question	Response
Kindly provide an overview of your family history. For example, was there an entrepreneur in your family? Did your family history influence your decision to start a business?	My family history was made up of workers. There were no entrepreneurs in my family, nor any college graduates. I am the first to think outside the box, wanting more than a paycheck. My family did influence my decision to start a business because I wanted more than I had seen or experienced.
What was your educational background? Do you have specific views on formal versus informal education? What are your views on Native American entrepreneurial training programs? Has education contributed to your business success?	My educational background includes my undergrad in business, and I am currently completing my coursework to obtain my master's in social work. Any type of education is a gift. I think there is a lot to be said about the benefits of informal education. To learn hands-on from others with first-hand experience is priceless; however, formal education will allow you to become a textbook expert in your field, which is required for better jobs and financial compensation. Overall, both formal and informal education are vital to your success.
Everyone has at least one role model, someone they aspire to be like. Do you have one who is an entrepreneur? How did the role model(s) influence your decision to start a business?	One of my role models was [Name]. She was an entrepreneur in the aspect of her activism. She suffered such great tragedy, yet she never gave up her fight to stand up and be brave. She became a writer and published multiple books. She influenced my decision to start a business of my own from her tireless effort to move forward. Reinforcing my dreams of not walking in the footsteps of followers but making my own path.
Starting a new business is not an easy process. What motivated you to start one? What steps did you take to start the business?	What motivated me to start my own business was by seeing and hearing from others how much their years of service had not been fulfilling to them. They may have a retirement after working 40 years, but they were often 40 unhappy years of working simply to receive their paycheck. I talked to others, I made a business plan (very small one), and I told myself to just start somewhere.

What challenges did you face when building your business, and how did you overcome them? Did you come across any unique circumstances as a result of your race?	The challenges of not having a guaranteed paycheck and the uncertainty of not knowing how successful I would be made me want to work harder. There have been multiple instances where I have experienced unique circumstances because of my race and appearance. They have ranged from negative to positive on the spectrum with curiosity and many judgments.
What types of support were most helpful to you when you were building your business? For example, did your local community play a role in shaping your business interests and development, or maybe it was a mentor? What or who was the one thing that made you believe, "Yes, I can do this!"	The most helpful support was people that believed in me and people I could be completely honest with that would help me talk through my plans. Advice from others is one of the most valuable tools you will receive. Accept it with grace and respect and then decide what to do with it.
What do you think are the essential skills needed for Native American entrepreneurs to succeed in America? Also, what personal attitudes do you think are essential?	I think Native American entrepreneurs need to be brave, educated, and passionate about their brand. They need to be confident and surround themselves with trusted and accountable people in their circle.
If you had the chance to start over again, would you do anything differently? If so, what's the reason?	Yes, I would have started sooner.
How would you characterize the state of Native American entrepreneurship in the United States? For instance, is it in the early stages, is it growing, or is it mature? Do you think it is open to all, or limited to certain individuals? Is it viable from anywhere in the country, or more favorable in certain states?	I think Native American entrepreneurship is growing; it makes me happy to see more and more business out there, native owned. It is growing and has decades to mature. What we need to do, is keep up with competitors by using technology the way they do. I think it is definitely limited in Indian Country, and will always be. Regardless, that will not stop us from growing our native businesses.
Are you a member of business organizations? Are these organizations unique to Native Americans or open to all races? Did they contribute to your business success?	I am not a member of business organizations today. I think most are open to all races, with the curiosity and interest of nonnatives about our culture and brands; we must be open to crossing the line and be available for all races. Certain states such as travel and tourist regions are definitely more accessible and sought after for native business sales.

(continued)

Question	Response
Do you think social networks and personal connections are important to business? Did you use networking when building your business, and are your social networks race based?	I do think social networks and personal connections are important. That is the way of our world today, and native business need to be aware of this and grow with it.
If you could give advice to young Native American entrepreneurs or other young people thinking about starting a business, what would be the most important consideration and why?	Know your passion, follow your dreams, and just start, now.
Have you been involved in socio-civic organizations or philanthropic work? If so, in which organizations, and what role did you play?	I have been involved with philanthropic work for years, I worked in Indian Country in Southern California as a hub between Corporate America and small nonprofit groups, I was co-chair of the Native American Professional Network in California (CA), and I have spent time volunteering across California, Charlotte, and Atlanta with United Way.
What do you see happening to your business in the future? Do you have succession plans in place? Do you see your business being run by family members or professional managers, and why?	Success, as I am always looking forward and thinking ahead. I think it is vital to have a backup plan and be realistic in business and dreamy in life. At some point, I would love my business to be run by professional managers that have experience being a leader. It is important to have a strong team backing you; you are as good as your team.
Where do you see yourself 10 years from now? What do you think is your legacy to the business community?	In 10 years, I would like to be independent and even more successful in my business. I am sure of my legacy in the business community, my name is known for my work, but I still have so much more work to do.

Entrepreneur 20: Tribal Affiliation—Sioux

Question	Response
Kindly provide an overview of your family history. For example, was there an entrepreneur in your family? Did your family history influence your decision to start a business?	Yes, my father was and still is a social entrepreneur.
What was your educational background? Do you have specific views on formal versus informal education? What are your views on Native American entrepreneurial training programs? Has education contributed to your business success?	I have a master's in business admin. My education gives me the knowledge I need to make my ideas work in the real world. I am able to talk shop with other business professionals because I have a formal education that prepared me to understand basic and complex business concepts.
Everyone has at least one role model, someone they aspire to be like. Do you have one who is an entrepreneur? How did the role model(s) influence your decision to start a business?	My dad is my role model.
Starting a new business is not an easy process. What motivated you to start one? What steps did you take to start the business?	Passion always drives my ideas.
What challenges did you face when building your business, and how did you overcome them? Did you come across any unique circumstances as a result of your race?	Access to capital is always a challenge for disenfranchised people of color. I overcame this by being creative and not taking no for an answer.
What types of support were most helpful to you when you were building your business? For example, did your local community play a role in shaping your business interests and development, or maybe it was a mentor? What or who was the one thing that made you believe, "Yes, I can do this!"	My mentors encouraged me and didn't let me give up.
What do you think are the essential skills needed for Native American entrepreneurs to succeed in America? Also, what personal attitudes do you think are essential?	Tenacity and thick skin. Being an entrepreneur isn't as glamorous as social media makes it look.

(continued)

Question	Response
If you had the chance to start over again, would you do anything differently? If so, what's the reason?	No
How would you characterize the state of Native American entrepreneurship in the United States? For instance, is it in the early stages, is it growing, or is it mature? Do you think it is open to all, or limited to certain individuals? Is it viable from anywhere in the country, or more favorable in certain states?	It's in its early stages but natives have been entrepreneurial since creation so it's woven into our DNA.
Are you a member of business organizations? Are these organizations unique to Native Americans or open to all races? Did they contribute to your business success?	I am a member of many organizations and they all contribute to my network— which is my net worth. ☺
Do you think social networks and personal connections are important to business? Did you use networking when building your business, and are your social networks race based?	Absolutely! In business, it's all about who you know!
If you could give advice to young Native American entrepreneurs or other young people thinking about starting a business, what would be the most important consideration and why?	Believe in what you are trying to do. No one is going to make it successful but YOU! No one is going to do you any favors, so be ready to work hard and learn every single day!
Have you been involved in socio-civic organizations or philanthropic work? If so, in which organizations, and what role did you play?	No
What do you see happening to your business in the future? Do you have succession plans in place? Do you see your business being run by family members or professional managers, and why?	I see my businesses thriving in the future. Most of my ventures are sole props, but AIBL definitely has a succession plan and will continue long after I'm gone.
Where do you see yourself 10 years from now? What do you think is your legacy to the business community?	I will be retired in 10 years but working harder than ever to create new solutions to challenges faced by our native communities!

This section included the results of 20 full interviews of Native American entrepreneurs from across the United States. The analysis of their responses is presented in the next section.

CHAPTER 4

Research Findings

If we wonder often, the gift of knowledge will come.

—Arapaho

This book is a product of extensive national research and analysis conducted by the authors.

While the gathered interviews are by no means conclusive, and only constitute a small sample of the population, there have been observable patterns and commonalities in the responses. The insights provided show an unprecedented view into the mind and psyche of the Native American entrepreneur.

The insights gathered offers value to many segments of society, including entrepreneurs of all races, corporate executives, government officials, academics, policymakers, and even international organizations.

It is noteworthy to mention that the captured mindset of the Native American entrepreneurs correspond to the year 2018 to 2019. Since cultures and attitudes do change over time, future and updated studies would be beneficial.

Descriptive coding, referred to 'highlighted responses' was used to narrow the findings and focus to illustrate synthesized evidence. According to Saldana (2009), descriptive coding is used to "summarize in a word or short phrase the basic topic of passage of qualitative data" (p. 70). This coding style was used to gain further understanding of the common entrepreneurial phenomenon.

The respondents come from different tribes and have a fairly balanced gender distribution. Attribute Tables 1 and 2 provide highlights of the participants in the study.

Attribute Table 1 Research participants

Participant pseudonym	Gender	Ethnicity	Tribal affiliation
Entrepreneur 1	Female	Native American	Quechan
Entrepreneur 2	Male	Native American	Sage, Potawatomi, Delaware
Entrepreneur 3	Female	Native American	Tsuut'ina
Entrepreneur 4	Female	Native American	Seminole
Entrepreneur 5	Female	Native American	Mohican, Delaware
Entrepreneur 6	Female	Native American	Quechan
Entrepreneur 7	Male	Native American	Navajo
Entrepreneur 8	Male	Native American	Ho-Chunk
Entrepreneur 9	Male	Native American	Seminole
Entrepreneur 10	Male	Native American	Chickasaw
Entrepreneur 11	Male	Native American	Caddo of Oklahoma
Entrepreneur 12	Male	Native American	Quechan
Entrepreneur 13	Female	Native American	Quechan
Entrepreneur 14	Male	Native American	Oglala Sioux
Entrepreneur 15	Female	Native American	Diné (Navajo)
Entrepreneur 16	Male	Native American	Quechan
Entrepreneur 17	Male	Native American	Chumash
Entrepreneur 18	Male	Native American	Quechan
Entrepreneur 19	Female	Native American	Yaqui
Entrepreneur 20	Female	Native American	Sioux

Attribute Table 2 Research participants synthesis

Gender	Ethnicity	Gender of Participants (%)
Female	Native American	9/20 (45%)
Male	Native American	11/20 (55%)

In this section, the questions asked, and a summary of the responses are organized into Summary Tables 1 to 15. A questionnaire assessment is offered to offer context and analysis of the responses.

Hereunder are our highlights of our findings.

Summary Table 1 Role of family in entrepreneurial decision

Question	Highlights of responses
Role of family in entrepreneurial decision	• Mother was an influence • Family members were not an influence • Parents were entrepreneurial • Father was entrepreneurial • Both parents were successful entrepreneurs • Tough conditions were a catalyst for the mother and family to be hard working and entrepreneurial

Questionnaire Assessment

Majority of the interviewees noted that family members, especially parents, were influential in their entrepreneurial decision. The entrepreneurial inclinations of the parents, along with the support and encouragement they provided, served as an impetus for the interviewees to engage in business. The results of the interviews underscore the influence that family role models play an important role in shaping the entrepreneurial propensity of Native American entrepreneurs.

Summary Table 2 Role of education in business success

Question	Highlights of responses
Role of education in business success	• Had a high school degree and some college credits • Challenges during college years spurred entrepreneurial drive • Undergraduate and postgraduate degrees enhanced perception of the world in a native and nonnative context • Education provides the foundation for dealing with new ways of life and intricacies of business • Graduated from high school and learned from life experiences • Job training was helpful in my education • Obtained a master's degree and found that formal education opened many doors and contributed to my success • Native American entrepreneurial training programs would be very beneficial to many • Certain degrees and programs such as trade or banking and finance can be more influential toward business success • Education provides the foundation to initiate change • Education is important but not critical to business success • Many natives monetize their talents but lack basic business fundamentals to grow as an entrepreneur • Getting a professional license can help one stand out • Education is important, but know it's not for everyone

Question	Highlights of responses
	• Education is a success contributor, but experience has significant weight as well
	• The degree I have was helpful, but not a necessity
	• A mentor is just as valuable as a professor when it comes to on-the-job training
	• Knowledge sets the foundation for empowerment of tribal members
	• Formal and informal education created the opportunity to look through various lenses that is essential in launching an enterprise
	• Education has given me more confidence and allowed me to harness my skills in research, communication, and other skill sets that are important for business success
	• Native American entrepreneurial programs are important because they could be the sole form of business education for many
	• Education should be a balance between formal and informal education
	• Many tribal people are already entrepreneurs, and they don't even know it. Taking an entrepreneurship training class will help cultivate organizational skills and provide a path toward profitability
	• Education should be complemented with hard work and the ability to make sound business decisions
	• Both formal and informal education are vital to success—informal education gets you the hands-on and first-hand experience; formal education helps you develop the expertise to eventually earn better financial compensation
	• Postgraduate education gave me the knowledge to make ideas work, understand basic and complex business concepts, and communicate effectively with other business professionals

Questionnaire Assessment

The interviewees had a wide range of educational qualifications ranging from high school to postgraduate studies. The findings suggest that absence of a degree in higher education is not a barrier for entrepreneurial leanings and success of the Native American entrepreneur. Some of the entrepreneurs highlighted the importance of life experiences, job training, mentors, and entrepreneurship training programs in entrepreneurial success. Those who pursued higher education saw value in the development of cross-cultural perspectives, acquisition of important business skills such as business research and communication, management of business complexities, network expansion, openness toward change, and the gaining of confidence. The formally educated entrepreneurs saw education as a platform for personal and professional growth as well as the gaining of management and business competencies essential for entrepreneurial success. One interviewee pointed out that there must be a balance between formal and informal education. The interviews suggest that Native American entrepreneurs place value on both formal and informal education.

Summary Table 3 Person who served as role model

Question	Highlights of responses
Person who served as role model	• Cousin served as role model • Don't have a role model—I admire certain people, but none really influenced me as role model • Mother and former chief provided the right values, motivation, and entrepreneurial ideas • Family history and lineage served as an entrepreneurial inspiration • Father was a role model—he had confidence and was willing to take risk • Business owner and former rapper was a role model • Mother was a role model—she instilled confidence and positive outlook • An entrepreneur who runs a communications firm consisting of several indigenous professionals • Role models are highly successful entrepreneurs who had foresight, global mindset, and pursued what they love • A former employer guided and developed me and empowered me to succeed • Parents were role models—dad had entrepreneurial spirit and bright outlook, and mom was a workaholic • Brother—he was successful, educated, and hard working • An entrepreneur activist—she rose from tragedy and never gave up

Questionnaire Assessment

The interviewees had a diverse opinion on who served as a role model. Their choices ranged from parents, sibling, cousin, chief, former employers, and successful entrepreneurs. Their desired attributes can be categorized into three types: doing (**Hands**), thinking (**Head**), and feeling (**Spirit**). The attribute relating to **Hands** include hard work. Attributes associated with **Head** include foresight, having a global mindset, being well-educated, and having positive outlook. The **Spirit** attributes are as follows: passionate with their work, possessing entrepreneurial drive, possessing confidence, having the courage to take risk, and providing support for the tribe. The interviews suggest that Native American entrepreneurs place high regard on an individual's ability to make good use of **Hands, Head,** and **Spirit.**

Summary Table 4 Drivers and steps for business start-up

Question	Highlights of responses
Drivers and steps for business start-up	• Hunger to have more for my children spurred a planning process that led to enterprise creation • Cared about people and enjoyed communicating—leveraged these to do artistic and entrepreneurial activities • Wanted to have a better future for my son and stirred entrepreneurial spirit • Saw a need and filled that need • Learned from others, then got inspired to do something similar on my own • Witnessed a friend succeed in business and decided to pursue a similar path • Noticed a major community need and decided to do something about it by leveraging networks and resources and creating a business plan • Found an opportunity to leverage technology to enhance communication within the tribe and subsequently started a business from it • Attracted by the market size of the industry and leveraged my skills to start selling products at Etsy • An MBA degree and a participant in a business plan competition set the foundation for me to pursue a low-risk, e-commerce strategy to sell products online • Built upon my passion for computers and information technology and created an enterprise • Desire for flexibility in work schedule set the stage for a business start-up • Had a mentor who taught me the business, and eventually I learned enough to start one on my own • Developed a plan to start the enterprise and built as much knowledge and information as possible on the business and industry • Seen and heard about the unhappiness of some people who simply worked for companies all their lives—decided to write a business plan to start somewhere • A passion and an idea led me to start an enterprise

Questionnaire Assessment

The interviewees decided to start an enterprise based on either a personal or an external catalyst. A personal catalyst is demonstrated by a statement like *desire to have more for my children.* An external catalyst was shown in a statement like *mentor taught me the business.* There were eight noted drivers for the enterprise start-up: (1) **Financial** (i.e., desire to have more for my children, wanted to have a better future for my son), (2) **Altruism** (i.e., cared about people in my community), (3) **Opportunity recognition** (i.e., saw a need and filled it, found an opportunity to leverage technology, saw the market size), (4) **Inspirational** (i.e., witnessed a friend succeed, had an idea and passion for it), (5) **Work–life balance** (i.e., desire for flexibility in work schedule), (6) **Encouragement** (i.e., mentor taught me the business), (7) **Goal driven** (i.e., developed a plan to start an enterprise, and (8) **Desire for change** (i.e., heard about unhappiness of those employed). The interviews suggest that there are many situations and events that can prompt the start of an entrepreneurial journey of a Native American entrepreneur.

Summary Table 5 Challenges faced when starting the business

Question	Highlights of responses
Challenges faced when starting the business	• Not believing in myself, self-doubt • Loathe paperwork • Circumstances relating to tribal background • Lack of financial knowledge • Balancing time between employment and the enterprise • Managing slow growth • Being comfortable with making a profit—as this is in conflict with tribal values • Lot of work • Balancing personal and professional time • Marketing to the right target market • Too much competition • Limited market since customers were all native • Financing and raising capital • Fear of unexpected market demand • Fear of customer rejection • Unsure whether to include race in the marketing process • Marketing and social media expansion • Finding top quality mentors, especially those outside of the Native American race • Developing proper communication skills • Learning how to network • Working through gender biases • Building a strong reputation • Race-related issues and biases • Getting the word out about your business • Financial uncertainty

Questionnaire Assessment

The interviewees faced a broad range of challenges when starting their businesses. These challenges can be categorized into four types: **Psychological**, **Developmental**, **Operational**, and **Environmental**. **Psychological** challenges refer to mindset and psyche of the entrepreneur and include concerns such as self-doubt, fear of the unexpected, fear of customer rejection, concern about financial uncertainty. **Developmental** challenges refer to areas where the entrepreneur may need to personally grow and include concerns such as interracial relationship building, management of paperwork, financial acumen, accessing mentors, communication skills, networking skills, working with gender biases, and reputation and brand building. **Operational** challenges refer to the modalities in which the entrepreneur can manage the business better and include concerns such as managing time and workload, growing the enterprise, effective marketing, and financing. **Environmental** challenges relate to external factors that impact venture viability and include concerns such as too much competition and limited market size. The interviews suggest that Native American entrepreneurs face **Psychological**, **Developmental**, **Operational**, and **Environmental** challenges when starting an enterprise and need to address these concerns in order to be successful.

Summary Table 6 Support provider for the start-up

Question	Highlights of responses
Support provider for the start-up	• Moral support from children • Words of encouragement from others • Companies that provided the first break • Support from organizations that supported indigenous businesses • Support from community • Savings and full-time employment provided financial stability • Mother • Support from local businesses and organizations • Husband and family members • Accountant • Academic institution and formal training • Boss • Support from nonprofit, professional, and civic organizations

Question	Highlights of responses
	• Research information and support • Investor • Availability of top talent • Tribal community support • Network • Professional training programs • Friends • Social media • Technological support • Local government and industry • Mentors

Questionnaire Assessment

The interviews suggest that the entrepreneurs benefitted from a broad range of support providers when they embarked on their entrepreneurial journey. These venture supporters can be classified into five types: **Family**, **Business**, **Community**, **Academic Institutions**, and **Government**. Mentioned supporters in the **Family** category included children, mother, and spouse. Supporters in the **Business** category included professionals (i.e., accountant), employer, employees, investor, research provider, tech provider, and mentors. Supporters in the **Community** category included civic organizations, tribe, network, friends, and social media. Supporters in the **Academic** community included academic institutions and training program providers. Cited supporters in the **Government** category largely comprised of the local government. It is evident from the interviews that Native American entrepreneurs rarely operate as an "island"; instead, they collaborate and work with multiple persons and organizations to advance their entrepreneurial goals.

Summary Table 7 Essential skills for success in America

Question	Highlights of responses
Essential skills for success in America	• Leveraging relationships with local tribe • Developing relationships with funders • Openness to change • Self-confidence • Being opportunistic • Understand there are no shortcuts to success

(continued)

Question	Highlights of responses
	• Don't be over-reliant on government • Approach business not as a Native American, but as a business person • Positive attitude • Willingness to learn and to teach • Learn from and work with others • Develop strong business skills • Find a healthy balance between traditional knowledge and formal education; cultural competency • Gain proper formal education • Speak the same language as mainstream society • Confidence • Self-reliance • Stay strong despite failures; grit; networking—inside and outside of the tribe • Ability to sell and market • Comfortable with taking risks • Being independent • Persuasiveness • Ability to negotiate • Creativity • Perseverance, resilience, persistence, tenacity • Ability to raise capital • Leadership • Character • Financial savvy • Treating other people well; emotional intelligence; be generous; give back • Positive attitude • Gathering community support • Business acumen • Research skills • Hard work • Humility • Become a movement for change • Proactiveness • Continuous education • Professionalism • Good communication skills • Self-discipline • Learn when to ask for help • Know your roots • Be passionate in what you do • Be courageous

Questionnaire Assessment

In the view of the interviewees, success in America is based on **Attitudinal**, **Developmental**, and **Operational** attributes. **Attitudinal** attributes refer to characteristics deemed essential to business success and included cross-cultural competency, openness to change, self-confidence, positive attitude, and self-discipline. **Developmental** attributes refer to essential skills and competencies such as obtaining formal education, research skills, communication skills, financial acumen, and continuous education. **Operational** attributes refer to practical approaches seen as important to organizational functions such as don't take shortcuts in business dealings, don't be over-reliant on the government, and plan ahead for capital-raising approaches. The interviews suggest that a broad range of skills and abilities are essential for business success of Native Americans in the United States and many of these are anchored in positive personal attitudes, a growth mindset, and sound business judgment.

Summary Table 8 Would you do things differently?

Question	Highlights of responses
Would you do things differently?	• No, all things happen for a reason • Yes, spent too little time building relationships • Yes, would start my business off reservation lands • Yes, would have engaged the SBA and similar organizations for funding • Yes, I would have tried to be a formal or informal mentor to a Native American academic consulting organization • No, everything I have done has led me to where I am today • Yes, I would put more value on my work rather than marketing myself as a commodity • Yes, never buy a yellow page ad ever again—they don't work • Yes, mistakes are made every day—we all learn from it • Yes, I would start smaller and build an audience • Yes, I would focus more on a strong financial foundation • Yes, I would try other options for products to sell • Yes, I would do better planning • Yes, I should have studied financial literacy early on • Yes, I would be better organized • Yes, I would use the nine years given by the SBA differently—learn quicker to under-promise and over-deliver • No, I am happy where I am with my business • Yes, I would start sooner • No, all has been good

Questionnaire Assessment

A majority of the respondents questioned, or 85 percent, thought they would do things differently. Only 15 percent indicated that they would do things the same way. The reasons cited by those who would keep things the same were anchored in the acknowledgment on the role of fate and destiny in one's life as well as satisfaction on where things are. As for those who would do things differently, their reasons were **strategic** (i.e., *engage organizations for funding*), **developmental** (i.e., *study financial literacy*), and **altruistic** (i.e., *would have tried to be a mentor*). The results of the interviews suggest that a majority of Native American entrepreneurs when looking at past events tend to pick up on areas for business, personal, and community improvement.

Summary Table 9 State of Native American entrepreneurship in the United States

Question	Highlights of responses
State of Native American Entrepreneurship in the United States	• Not sure, there's no data • Early stages, it needs more time to develop and evolve • Timing is tremendous for Native Americans and all other entrepreneurs • Don't know—it hasn't changed much, don't see it growing • Early stages • It is growing and spreading • Could use more support from their tribal nation • It is gaining momentum, but not at a rate other races have • The future looks good—with better laws alongside the resiliency and knowledge in our elders with a very energetic youth • It is just the tip of the iceberg of what we are capable of • It is blossoming with the rise of social media, access to broader audiences that can motivate anyone to start a business • It is growing as more natives get educated • It is growing and the potential is in the urban areas on the West and East Coasts as well as online • It is growing and with an exciting and attractive growth rate • Native entrepreneurship in the United States and beyond has yet to be tapped, which has excellent prospects for job creation and revenue generation • It has grown and government contracting has had a huge revenue boost for tribes everywhere • Not sure—I believe it remains challenging for those living on or near a reservation • It is growing and can further mature in decades to come, especially with all the technological breakthroughs around • It's in the early stages, but the growth prospect is there since natives have always been entrepreneurial; its woven in the DNA.

Questionnaire Assessment

Approximately 15 percent of the interviewees were uncertain or unsure of the current state of Native American entrepreneurship in the United States. The rest of the interviewees, or 85 percent, believed Native American entrepreneurship is either in its early stages or still growing. One interviewee mentioned that the state of entrepreneurship for Native Americans needs more time to develop and evolve. Another interviewee indicated that we have only witnessed the 'tip of the iceberg' of indigenous entrepreneurship. Majority of the interviewees have a positive outlook for the future citing better laws, market expansion, opportunities in government contracting, dynamism of the youth, access to education, social media, and technological breakthroughs as catalysts for new entrepreneurial prospects. One interviewee pointed out that significant growth will likely be in the urban areas in the West and East Coasts as well as online. The interviews suggest that majority of Native American entrepreneurs believe there is room for further growth and business development in the United States.

Summary Table 10 Membership in business organizations and its role in success

Question	Highlights of responses
Membership in business organizations and its role in success	• No, but I can see the value • No, not a member but with working relationship • Yes, and its open to all races • Yes, American Indian Business Leaders organization • Yes, local chamber of commerce • No • Yes, Native American Chamber of Commerce • Yes, several civic and business organizations have contributed to my business success • Yes, National Center for American Indian Enterprise Development • Yes—the American Indian Chamber of Commerce has been great • Yes, through LinkedIn I'm open to all organizations • Yes, several organizations catering to several races • No • Yes, business and professional organizations open to all races—gained clients through them and learned more about business • No, but I see the potential • Yes • No • No—but I think it's an important way to mingle with all races • Yes, and it contributed to my network and net worth

Questionnaire Assessment

As much as 30 percent of Native American entrepreneurs were not involved in business organizations. Some of these respondents, while not currently involved in organizations, understand the potential and see the value. The majority, or 70 percent, who are involved in organizations generally claimed that memberships in these organizations impacted their business success. While several interviewees were largely involved with Native American or tribal organizations, many participated in non–race-based groups. The benefits associated with membership include network expansion, professional development, and business generation.

Summary Table 11 Importance of social networks in business

Question	Highlights of responses
Importance of social networks in business	• Yes, it is important • My business relies on it • Relationship building is key • Social, academic, and native relationships can be pathways to partnerships • It is not something one is entitled to; you have to work at it • Personal relationships and social networks are vital to business success • Combine physical and digital social networking • Social relationships are important not only for business development but also as a means to recruit top talent • Know the niche and most impactful segment to cultivate relationships • Business is all about who you know

Questionnaire Assessment

All of the interviewed Native American entrepreneurs indicated that one's social network is instrumental to business success. The benefits associated with social networks include business generation, partnership development, and recruitment of talent. One respondent mentioned the importance of blending both physical and digital platforms when developing one's network. Advice offered by the entrepreneurs included using technology to optimize networking, working hard at it, and finding a unique niche to focus networking efforts. The interview results suggest that several Native American entrepreneurs are strategically using social networking as a tool to help grow their business.

Summary Table 12 Advice to young Native American entrepreneurs

Question	Highlights of responses
Advice to young Native American entrepreneurs	• There will be roadblocks; remember that your loved ones are there to keep you going • Focus on getting things done • Manage your financials well • Do what you love • Do your research and understand your demographics well • Educate yourself • Work hard • Develop cross-cultural skills • Don't be afraid to fail • Dream big • Understand where you add value—what problem are you really solving? • Pick an industry with fewer competitors • Write a business plan • Utilize free and personal resources • Find a good mentor—be open to getting coached • Learn and perform • Listen and ask good questions • Persevere • Develop a vision and mission • Learn about business early in life • Know what you're passionate about • Believe in yourself and your dream

Questionnaire Assessment

The interviewees offered a broad range of advice to younger Native Americans. The advice can be categorized into three types: **Attitudinal**, **Developmental**, and **Operational**. The **Attitudinal** advice pertains to attributes deemed essential for success and included: work hard, dream big, and believe in yourself. The **Developmental** advice relate to obtaining skill sets to improve oneself and included learning cross-cultural skills, educate oneself, and learn to manage financials.

The **Operational** advice were essential organizational strategies and included: know where you add value, write a plan, and utilize free resources. The interviews suggest that there are multiple pathways for young Native Americans to succeed in business, and they are anchored in cultivating the right attitude, developing oneself, and implementing sound business practices.

Summary Table 13 Involvement in socio-civic and philanthropic work

Question	Highlights of responses
Involvement in socio-civic and philanthropic work	• No • Yes, UNITY—United Indian Tribal Youth • Yes—involved with tribal government work and nonprofits • Yes—Professional Growth for Women in Business • Yes—work with several social and philanthropic organizations • Yes—I have a leadership role at the National American Indian Business Leaders • Not really involved—but collaborated with nonprofits • Yes—leadership roles in several socio-civic organizations • Not recently • Yes—church and several other groups • Yes—currently president of an honor society • Yes—helped in a program that implemented native support initiatives • Yes, volunteered for several years with the NCAIED's RES • Yes—I was involved with the NACA • Yes—several organizations such as the Indian Country in Southern California and the Native American Professional Network

Questionnaire Assessment

As much as 30 percent of the interviewed Native American entrepreneurs claimed they were not involved in socio-civic or philanthropic work. A vast majority, or 70 percent, however, were involved in a wide range of organizations, including both race and non-race-based groups. Some of the interviewees held leadership roles in the organizations with which they were associated. The interviews suggest that despite the demanding work load of entrepreneurs, many Native American entrepreneurs find the time to engage in socio-civic work and give back to the local community.

Summary Table 14 Perception of business in the future

Question	Highlights of responses
Perception of business in the future	• Expanding around the world • Move from sole proprietorship to nonprofit • Want to be the Ted Talk for Native people in North America • See the business growing successfully and rapidly • I plan to keep working while I like it—retirement is still many years from now • I see the business growing and thriving • I plan to grow my team, and I have a succession plan in place • The business will grow rapidly in the near term—don't see involvement from family members • Positive outlook—but proper planning is important • Geographic expansion as well as product type offering • I see the business as accomplishing great things and making an impact • More service offering and greater involvement of the community • Revitalize my business and have greater confidence • Strategic hiring to boost marketing and pursue related start-up ventures • Recruit a professional management team to pursue growth and development • Have a retirement plan • I may sell the business or have the children run it • I'll be realistic and have a backup plan • I have a strong succession plan for my businesses so they can continue long after I'm gone

Questionnaire Assessment

All of the respondents had a positive outlook of the future. A majority of the interviewed entrepreneurs, or 60 percent, talked about expanding or further growing the business. Only a small portion, or 10 percent, spoke of retirement, suggesting most had an inclination to keep on working much later in life. About 15 percent talked about a succession plan, and approximately the same percentage of participants discussed a back-up plan. The interviews suggest that while Native American entrepreneurs tend to encompass diverse approaches toward business development in the future, a common thread is a positive outlook and optimism to take their venture into new heights.

Summary Table 15 Perception of future self and legacy

Question	Highlights of responses
Perception of future self and legacy	• Traveling the world and impacting lives • Need to set up plans with spouse—will have to think about "we" rather than just "me" • I'd like to be active in economic development as advisor or CEO of a tribal organization • Established business with franchises • Publish books and articles that will help the future generation • Much stronger business expertise • Amassing significant wealth and making in-roads for my race as well as my industry • Amazing wealth and fame while advancing the needs of indigenous communities • Retired and being a subject matter expert • Do tribal diagnostics and make an impact on the economy and health of tribes • Give other Native Americans opportunities in business • Seeing my work make an impact on the tribal community as well as the Indian Country • Changing the way our history is portrayed in media and schools, and helping make policy changes • Working with the government to help improve lives in tribal communities • Retired and have successfully hired and trained young native people and develop them into successful professionals and businesspeople • A leader in my industry and helping develop the economic development of Indian Reservations • I am hoping to retire early and share my knowledge with others • Encourage others to learn their language and culture • Still in business and helping others understand government contracting • Retired and getting my companies involved by volunteering in community work • Hoping my business has made a significant impact on the community • Independent and become even more successful in business • Retired and working harder to find solutions to challenges faced in our native communities

Questionnaire Assessment

The interviewees had diverse views on future plans and legacy. In their responses, only a small number, or 20 percent, spoke of retirement. An even smaller number, or 10 percent, framed their response on wealth creation. Approximately 20 percent wanted to try something new; most intended to stay the course and grow the business. A large majority, or 70 percent, focused their response on giving back or making a significant impact on their tribe, the Native American community, as well as the local, national, and global communities. The interviews suggest that many Native American entrepreneurs are deeply motivated to help and support their communities and have made this a goal in their future plans. This common outlook suggests that the fundamental ideas of collectivism are well-engrained within Native American culture as most entrepreneurs sought to embrace, protect, and support their community.

The interviews underscore the following key findings:

1. **Role model**—family role models play an important role in shaping the entrepreneurial propensity of Native American entrepreneurs.
2. **Role of education**—Native American entrepreneurs place value on both formal and informal education.
3. **Ideal role models**—Native American entrepreneurs place high regard on an individual's ability to make good use of **Hands**, **Head**, and **Spirit**.
4. **Drivers for enterprise start-up**—there were eight noted drivers for the enterprise start-up: (1) **Financial** (i.e., desire to have more for my children; wanted to have a better future for my son), (2) **Altruism** (i.e., cared about people in my community), (3) **Opportunity recognition** (i.e., saw a need and filled it; found an opportunity to leverage technology; saw the market size), (4) **Inspirational** (i.e., witnessed a friend succeed; had an idea and passion for it), (5) **Work–life balance** (i.e., desire for flexibility in work schedule), (6) **Encouragement** (i.e., mentor taught me the business), (7) **Goal driven** (i.e., developed a plan to start an enterprise), and (8) **Desire for change** (i.e., heard about unhappiness of those employed).

5. **Challenges in the enterprise start-up**—Native American entrepreneurs face **Psychological, Developmental, Operational**, and **Environmental** challenges when starting an enterprise and need to address these concerns in order to be successful.

6. **Supporters of enterprise start-up**—venture supporters can be classified into five types: **Family, Business, Community, Academic Institutions**, and **Government.**

7. **Essential skills for success**—success for Native Americans in the United States is anchored in **Attitudinal, Developmental**, and **Operational** attributes. A broad range of skills and abilities are essential for business success of Native Americans, and many of these are anchored in positive personal attitudes, a growth mindset, and sound business judgment.

8. **Areas for change**—majority of the Native American entrepreneurs thought they would do things differently in business. Their reasons were **strategic** (i.e., *engage organizations for funding*), **developmental** (i.e., *study financial literacy*), and **altruistic** (i.e., *would have tried to be a mentor*).

9. **State of Native American entrepreneurship**—majority of the entrepreneurs believe that Native American entrepreneurship is either in its early stages or still growing. They believe there is room for further growth and business development in the United States.

10. **Role of business organizations**—the majority of the Native American entrepreneurs were involved in organizations and claimed that membership impacted their business success. The cited benefits associated with membership include network expansion, professional development, and business generation.

11. **Importance of social networks**—all of the interviewed Native American entrepreneurs indicated that one's social network is instrumental to business success.

12. **Advice to young Native American entrepreneurs**—the advice was categorized into three types: **Attitudinal, Developmental**, and **Operational**. There are multiple pathways for young Native Americans to succeed in business, and they are anchored in cultivating the right attitude, developing oneself, and implementing sound business practices.

13. **Involvement in socio-civic and philanthropic work**—a majority of Native American entrepreneurs were involved in a wide range of organizations, including both race and non-race-based groups. Despite the demanding work load of entrepreneurs, many Native American entrepreneurs find the time to engage in socio-civic work and give back to the local community.

14. **Perception of future business**—the Native American entrepreneurs had a positive outlook of the future and a majority of them talked about expanding or further growing the business. While Native American entrepreneurs tend to take on diverse approaches toward business development in the future, a common thread is a positive outlook and optimism to take their venture into new heights.

15. **Perception of future self and legacy**—the Native American entrepreneurs have diverse views on future plans and legacy. A large majority of them focused their response on giving back or making a significant impact on their tribe, the Native American community, as well as the local, national, and global communities. The interviews suggest that many Native American entrepreneurs are deeply motivated to help and support their communities and have made this a goal in their future plans.

The findings underscore the fact that Native American entrepreneurship is alive and well in the United States in contemporary times. Like all other entrepreneurs, they are driven to make their business efforts work. They pursue a multitude of strategies and engage multiple parties to advance their goals. Native American entrepreneurs are an integral part of the tribal, national, and global communities that one day hope to make a positive impact in our society as a whole.

Reference

Saldana, J. 2009. *The Coding Manual for Qualitative Research*. Thousand Oaks, CA: Sage.

CHAPTER 5

Conclusions and Recommendations

We will be known forever by the tracks we leave.

—Dakota

The findings underscore the importance of support groups in the way Native American entrepreneurs carry out their business. Specifically, the identified areas of support include the following: **Family, Business, Community, Academic Institutions**, and **Government**.

In this conclusions and recommendations section, the authors revisit the key interview findings and offer specific suggestions in areas where the support groups can make an impact on the lives and businesses of Native American entrepreneurs.

Role of Family

Family members include parents (biological or guardian), spouse, siblings, and children. The interviews underscore the following key findings and their implications on the family:

Findings	Implications on the family
Family role models play an important role in shaping the entrepreneurial propensity of Native American entrepreneurs.	Parents in Native American households need to understand that the children learn from observing familial actions. A family that embraces and nurtures entrepreneurial values would likely have their children grown up to become entrepreneurs.
Native American entrepreneurs place value on both formal and informal education.	Given the importance of both formal and informal education to an entrepreneur's success, Native American families should consider supporting the educational aspirations of family members while embracing traditional tribal culture and customs.

Findings	Implications on the family
Native American entrepreneurs place high regard on an individual's ability to make good use of **Hands**, **Head**, and **Spirit**.	Native American entrepreneurs tend to value hard work, logic, as well as empathy for others. Family members should consider cultivating these values through tribal teachings and modern examples.
Financial motivation for the family was one of the drivers for the entrepreneurial start-up.	Family members need to understand that the long hours at work and the hard work of parents and spouses are driven by a desire for financial betterment for the family. Also, family members should recognize that the desire for financial betterment may not be rooted in the modern Western concepts of individualism.
Work–life balance was among the key reasons for an entrepreneurial start-up.	Life in corporate America can be very stressful for an individual and the family. Family members need to understand that a person's desire to be an entrepreneur can be based on the desire to spend more time for oneself and the family. In addition, in many cases, indigenous entrepreneurs often do not place enormous value on traditional U.S. hierarchical business structures that may prompt entrepreneurship.
Encouragement contributed to the entrepreneurial decision.	The family's support for and encouragement toward entrepreneurship can influence a family member's decision to start an enterprise.
Native American entrepreneurs face **Psychological** and **Developmental** challenges when starting an enterprise.	Family members need to understand that Native American entrepreneurs can be constrained by factors such as lack of confidence or inadequacy of education or skill. Providing encouragement and support for education can help family members achieve their entrepreneurial dreams.
Success for Native Americans in the United States is anchored in **Attitudinal** and **Developmental** attributes.	Family members should realize that the right attitude along with personal and professional development are foundations for entrepreneurial success.
Many Native American entrepreneurs see business organizations and social networks as essential for venture success.	Family members need to understand that while an entrepreneur's involvement in organizations may mean time away from the family, these efforts can lead to positive impact on the entrepreneur's business.

Findings	Implications on the family
Native American entrepreneurs tend to be involved in socio-civic and philanthropic organizations.	Family members need to understand that while socio-civic and philanthropic activities may mean time away from the family, it brings a sense of fulfillment and heightened self-worth for the entrepreneur.
Native American entrepreneurs think of their family as they envision their future self.	Native American entrepreneurs tend to put into consideration their spouses and children when they think of the future plans.

The findings highlight the large role the family plays in the Native American's business success. It is recommended that training providers, educational institutions, and policymakers take these important findings into account as developmental efforts are planned out for Native Americans in the United States.

Role of Business Community

The greater business community can learn much from a more indigenous perspective of trade and sustenance. Through making real and authentic connections with those business transactions, the ideas of entrepreneurship become more family oriented.

Morris (2002), posits:

> For members of ethnic groups, it would seem that values of the subculture could become internalized to the point that they affect entrepreneurial motives and behaviors. Thus, values of bravery, wisdom, or respect for earth shared by Native Americans might manifest themselves not only in career choices, but in the entrepreneur's approach to opportunity identification or network building. (p. 35)

The business community includes professionals (i.e., accountants), employers, research providers, consultants, investors, employees, tech providers, and mentors. The interviews underscore the following key findings and their implications on the business community:

Findings	Implications on the business community
Native American entrepreneurs place value on both formal and informal education.	Employers need to understand that Native Americans tend to value education as part of their professional growth. Mentors and education providers should realize that entrepreneurial success of Native Americans are linked to the kind of education they acquire.
Native American entrepreneurs place high regard on an individual's ability to make good use of **Hands**, **Head**, and **Spirit**.	Some members of the business community are role models to Native American Entrepreneurs. Highlighting values such as hard work, logic, and empathy would be helpful.
Work–life balance is a motivator for the entrepreneurial start-up.	Employers, investors, and service providers need to understand that many Native Americans seek to find a healthy work–life balance. In conjunction with possibly lowered appreciation for hierarchy within U.S. businesses, it's important for the business community to recognize a likely need for high levels of independence from native entrepreneurs.
Encouragement factored into the entrepreneurial decision.	Employers, investors, service providers, and mentors need to realize that words of encouragement can serve as a catalyst to a Native American's entrepreneurial decision.
Native American entrepreneurs face **Psychological**, **Developmental**, **Operational**, and **Environmental** challenges when starting an enterprise and need to address these concerns in order to be successful.	Investors, service providers, and mentors need to understand that Native American entrepreneurs face numerous challenges. Motivating them, helping them develop, providing assistance in operational challenges, and aiding them in the comprehension of environmental factors that can impact the business would be helpful.
Success for Native Americans in the United States is anchored in **Attitudinal**, **Developmental**, and **Operational** attributes.	Employers, investors, service providers, and mentors need to realize that nurturing values such as positive personal attitudes, a growth mindset, cultural acknowledgment, and sound business judgment can positively impact the Native American enterprise.

Findings	Implications on the business community
Native American entrepreneurs tend to want to improve on the following areas: strategic (i.e., engage organizations for funding), developmental (i.e., study financial literacy), and altruistic (i.e., would have tried to be a mentor).	Investors, service providers, and mentors need to assess how strategic approaches, personal development, and community linkages impact the venture and help it grow.
Many Native American entrepreneurs see business organizations and social networks as essential for venture success.	Employers, investors, service providers, and mentors should support the Native American entrepreneur's participation in business organizations and social networks because these activities could have a positive business impact.
Native American entrepreneurs tend to be involved in socio-civic and philanthropic organizations.	Employers, investors, service providers, and mentors should support the Native American entrepreneur's participation in socio-civic and philanthropic organizations since it provides a sense of fulfillment and self-worth for the individual.
Native American entrepreneurs had a positive outlook of the future, and a majority of them talked about expanding or further growing the business.	Employers, investors, service providers, and mentors need to understand that Native American entrepreneurs have an optimistic perspective of the future. This positive outlook can be built on to achieve entrepreneurial success.
Native American entrepreneurs are deeply motivated to help and support their communities and have made this a goal in their future plans.	Employers, investors, service providers, and mentors should realize that behind the Native American's entrepreneurial dream is to eventually give back to the community and provide a lasting legacy.

Currently, the business community provides support and countless resources to help the Native American entrepreneur succeed (Table 5.1).

It makes sense to utilize these resources when planning to grow the enterprise.

The findings underscore the important role the business community plays in the Native American's business success. It is recommended that training providers, educational institutions, and policymakers consider these findings as they plan a future for growth for Native American entrepreneurs.

Table 5.1 Business resources for Native American entrepreneurs

SBA business development programs	SBA provides access to business counseling, training, guidance, and contracts.
Grant funding	Grants are available for Native Americans from government and tribal organizations such as Montana Indian Equity Fund, Native American Venture Acceleration Fund (VAF) in New Mexico. The SBA office of Native American Affairs also offer grants.
Microloans	Accion offers small loans to entrepreneurs. There are flexible requirements, and one may still acquire a loan even with lack of credit history or poor credit.
Specialty organizations and nonprofits	There are several other organizations that assist Native American entrepreneurs such as Office of Native American Affairs, National Center for American Indian Enterprise Development, The First Nation Development Institute, and The American Indigenous Business Leaders.

Source: Accion.org (2018).

Role of Community (Other Stakeholders)

Other stakeholders in the Native American entrepreneur's world include civic organizations, tribe, network, friends, and social media circle. The interviews underscore the following key findings and their implications on other stakeholders:

Findings	Implications on other stakeholders
Native American entrepreneurs place value on both formal and informal education.	Civic organizations and tribal groups should provide a platform for educational access for Native Americans. Friends and the social media circle should encourage education among their peers.
Native American entrepreneurs place high regard on an individual's ability to make good use of **Hands**, **Head**, and **Spirit**.	Stakeholders in the Native American entrepreneur's circle should highlight values such as hard work, logic, and empathy.
Success of friends provides inspiration for entrepreneurial ventures.	Stakeholders in the Native American entrepreneur's circle should share success stories to stimulate entrepreneurial interest.

Findings	Implications on other stakeholders
Encouragement can lead to new venture formation.	Words of encouragement can inspire entrepreneurial initiatives.
Native American entrepreneurs face **Psychological, Developmental, Operational,** and **Environmental** challenges.	Stakeholders in the Native American entrepreneur's circle should find avenues to motivate peers, help others develop, provide guidance in operational challenges, and assist them in the comprehension of environmental factors that can impact the venture.
Success for Native Americans in the United States is anchored in **Attitudinal, Developmental,** and **Operational** attributes.	Stakeholders in the Native American entrepreneur's circle should find ways to develop positive personal attitudes, a growth mindset, and sound business judgment among their peers.
There is room for further growth and business development in Native American entrepreneurship in the United States.	Stakeholders in the Native American entrepreneur's circle should find ways to encourage entrepreneurship.
Native American entrepreneurs were involved in a wide range of organizations in the socio-civic and philanthropic space.	Stakeholders in the Native American entrepreneur's circle should embrace this involvement and strive to make a bigger impact on the well-being of the community.
Native American entrepreneurs tend to want to give back or make a significant impact on their tribe, the Native American community, as well as the local, national, and global communities.	Stakeholders in the Native American entrepreneur's circle should leverage this propensity for altruism and use this as a platform for community improvement.

It is clear from the findings that other stakeholders are influential and recipients of the Native American's business success. Supporting the efforts of the entrepreneurs can lead to significant betterment in the tribe, local, national, and even global communities. It is recommended that training providers, educational institutions, and policymakers consider these findings as they seek ways to advance Native American entrepreneurship.

Role of Academic Institutions

Academic institutions include colleges and universities as well as training providers that contributed knowledge to the Native American entrepreneur. The interviews highlight the following key findings and their implications on academic institutions and training organizations:

Findings	Implications on academic institutions
Family role models play an important role in shaping the entrepreneurial propensity of Native American entrepreneurs.	Providing for a learning platform for all Native American family members would have merit.
Native American entrepreneurs place value on both formal and informal education.	Planning for formal and informal entrepreneurship training programs for Native American entrepreneurs could provide unique advantages.
Native American entrepreneurs place high regard on an individual's ability to make good use of **Hands, Head,** and **Spirit.**	Integrating the values such as hard work, logic, and empathy in the curriculum would be helpful to Native American entrepreneurs.
There were eight noted drivers for the enterprise start-up: (1) **Financial** (i.e., desire to have more for my children; wanted to have a better future for my son), (2) **Altruism** (i.e., cared about people in my community), (3) **Opportunity recognition** (i.e., saw a need and filled it; found an opportunity to leverage technology; saw the market size), (4) **Inspirational** (i.e., witnessed a friend succeed; had an idea and passion for it), (5) **Work–life balance** (i.e., desire for flexibility in work schedule), (6) **Encouragement** (i.e., mentor taught me the business), (7) **Goal driven** (i.e., developed a plan to start an enterprise), (8) **Desire for change** (i.e., heard about unhappiness of those employed).	Integrating these eight drivers in Native American training and development programs would be beneficial.
Native American entrepreneurs face **Psychological, Developmental, Operational,** and **Environmental** challenges.	Addressing **Psychological, Developmental, Operational,** and **Environmental** challenges in Native American training and development programs could impact venture success.
Native American venture supporters include: **Family, Business, Community, Academic Institutions,** and **Government.**	Teaching Native American entrepreneurs how to gain optimal support from **Family, Business, Community, Academic Institutions,** and **Government** would be beneficial.

Findings	Implications on academic institutions
Success for Native Americans in the United States is anchored in **Attitudinal, Developmental**, and **Operational** attributes.	Helping Native American entrepreneurs learn positive personal attitudes, development of a growth mindset, and sound business judgment can contribute to venture success.
Native American entrepreneurs tend to want to improve on the following areas: **strategic** (i.e., *engage organizations for funding*), **developmental** (i.e., *study financial literacy*), and **altruistic** (i.e., *would have tried to be a mentor*).	Gaining knowledge on strategic venture approaches, personal development, and heightened community engagement would be helpful to the Native American entrepreneur.
There is room for further growth and business development in Native American entrepreneurship in the United States.	Educational institutions, both formal and informal, should encourage entrepreneurship among Native American entrepreneurs.
Many Native American entrepreneurs see business organizations and social networks as essential for venture success.	Educational institutions should include effective networking strategies in entrepreneurship training programs for Native American entrepreneurs.
Native American entrepreneurs tend to have a positive outlook of the future.	Educational institutions should build upon this positive outlook to encourage the pursuit of excellence and the attainment of entrepreneurial dreams.

The findings show that providers of formal and nonformal education to Native Americans have a large role to play in shaping their entrepreneurial skills and interest. An intentional effort should be outlined. Training programs tailored to address specific Native American challenges and opportunities would be very valuable in developing entrepreneurs. It is recommended that educational institutions, training providers, and policymakers consider these findings when educating the current and future Native American community.

Role of Government

The government has the dual role of impacting and being impacted by the entrepreneurial pursuits of the Native American community.

The interviews point out to the following key findings and their implications on the government:

Findings	Implications on government
Family role models play an important role in shaping the entrepreneurial propensity of Native American entrepreneurs.	When thinking of economic and business development programs for the Native American community, the government needs to understand that the family plays a central role.
Native American entrepreneurs place value on both formal and informal education.	There are multiple ways in which Native Americans can obtain their education. Any of these means can become a stimulus for entrepreneurial activity. Government programs and policies need to take these unique perspectives into account.
Native American entrepreneurs place high regard on an individual's ability to make good use of **Hands**, **Head**, and **Spirit**.	Government officials have the opportunity to learn from Native Americans. By recognizing a deeply engrained cultural awareness within Native America, government officials can embrace the changing landscape of American diversity and work to highlight entrepreneurial approaches based on land tenure, business survival techniques, hard work, logic, and empathy.
There were eight noted drivers for the enterprise start-up: (1) **Financial** (i.e., desire to have more for my children; wanted to have a better future for my son), (2) **Altruism** (i.e., cared about people in my community), (3) **Opportunity recognition** (i.e., saw a need and filled it; found an opportunity to leverage technology; saw the market size), (4) **Inspirational** (i.e., witnessed a friend succeed; had an idea and passion for it), (5) **Work–life balance** (i.e., desire for flexibility in work schedule), (6) **Encouragement** (i.e., mentor taught me the business), (7) **Goal driven** (i.e., developed a plan to start an enterprise), (8) **Desire for change** (i.e., heard about unhappiness of those employed).	Integrating these eight drivers in economic planning and policy formulation would be helpful.
Native American entrepreneurs face **Psychological, Developmental, Operational,** and **Environmental** challenges.	Addressing **Psychological, Developmental, Operational**, and **Environmental** challenges in economic planning and policy formulation could impact venture success.

Findings	Implications on government
Native American venture supporters include: **Family, Business, Community, Academic Institutions,** and **Government.**	The government has been identified as influential to venture success. Planning for programs and policies that stimulate entrepreneurship in communities can be beneficial for residents and the government as well.
Success for Native Americans in the United States is anchored in **Attitudinal, Developmental,** and **Operational** attributes.	Implementing policies and programs that help Native American entrepreneurs embrace positive personal perspectives, develop a growth mindset, and sound business judgment can strengthen entrepreneurship and improve the community.
Native American entrepreneurs tend to want to improve on the following areas: strategic (i.e., *engage organizations for funding*), developmental (i.e., *study financial literacy*), and altruistic (i.e., *would have tried to be a mentor*).	Developing policies and programs geared toward improving strategic venture approaches, personal development, and community engagement could stimulate entrepreneurship and strengthen the community.
There is room for further growth and business development in Native American entrepreneurship in the United States.	The government needs to realize that there is a potential for strengthening business and encouraging entrepreneurial growth in the Native American business community. Tapping into this opportunity can transform communities worldwide.
Native American entrepreneurs tend to have a positive outlook of the future.	The government should build upon this positive outlook to encourage community engagement and economic development.

The findings indicate that the government has an important role to play and can be a major beneficiary to the success of Native American entrepreneurs. Implementing policies and programs that support Native American entrepreneurship could transform communities, cities, states, and the entire country. This support should be tempered with a fundamental understanding that the very government that is now seeking to help was only very recently actively working to restrict indigenous economic prosperity. These deeply rooted emotions are still present within most indigenous people in North America and must be respected as foundational elements of a powerfully perseverant race.

This book captured the Native American entrepreneur psyche in the New Millennium. Today's business environment is very different from the time when indigenous people of this land nomadically embraced the earth and *successfully flourished for thousands of years* in a very different cultural climate.

Some values and business methodologies employed by Native Americans may have evolved with the advent of technological breakthroughs and heightened cross-cultural interactions. However, the essence of culture and tradition for indigenous people appears to remain the core elements of life, survival, and the very reason for entrepreneurial ventures.

The future looks bright for Native American entrepreneurs. Their ability to learn from tradition and merge those customs with modern and innovative ways provides them with an unparalleled perspective of business and life. Their perennially positive outlook provides a strong foundation for their entrepreneurial journey. Native American entrepreneurs are alive and well and are poised to redefine America in the coming years.

Entrepreneurship means something quite unique to most indigenous people. The commonly used idiom of *pulling yourself up by your own bootstraps*, which alludes to an oversimplified idea of self-improvement, is far from valid. The human experience continues to illustrate that entrepreneurship thrives with support and encouragement of others. Indigenous entrepreneurs remind us that all groups of people start their journey as part of a *tribe* and understand best that true success comes from shared wisdom.

References

Accion.org. 2018. "Business Resources for Native American Entrepreneurs." https://us.accion.org/resource/business-resources-native-american-entrepreneurs/, (accessed April 21, 2018).

Morris, M., M. Schindehutte, and J. Lesser. 2002. Ethnic Entrepreneurship: Do Values Matter? *New England Journal of Entrepreneurship* 5, no. 2, pp. 35–46. https://0-search-proquest-com.read.cnu.edu/docview/231141325?accountid=10100

About the Authors

Dr. Ron P. Sheffield is a member of the Fort Yuma Quechan (Kwatsáan) Indian Tribe of Arizona; adjunct professor of Leadership and American Studies at Christopher Newport University (CNU) located in Newport News, Virginia; president of OrgScience, Inc. (boutique management consulting firm); and a member of the board of directors for the American Indigenous Business Leaders (AIBL.org). He is an annually invited lecturer discussing, "Leadership Perspectives in Native America," "Abuse in Indian Country," and "Indigenous Perspective on Counseling" at the College of William & Mary in Williamsburg, Virginia, and Youngstown State University in Youngstown, Ohio. Ron's 2013 doctoral dissertation at the George Washington University in Washington, D.C., was completed on the Fort Yuma reservation and was titled, *The Influence of Language on Culture and Identity: Resurgence of the Quechan Native American Tribal Language* where respected Quechan tribal elders were interviewed as he sought to gain greater understanding of the influence that language restriction, and later legitimization by the U.S. federal government, had on tribal elder's individual perspectives of culture and identity.

Dr. J. Mark Munoz is a tenured full professor of International Business at Millikin University in Illinois and a former visiting fellow at the Kennedy School of Government at Harvard University. He is a recipient of several awards, including four best research paper awards, a literary award, international book awards, and the ACBSP Teaching Excellence Award among others. In 2016, he was recognized by the Academy of Global Business Advancement as Distinguished Business Dean, and in 2019 he received a Global Academic Excellence Award. Aside from top-tier journal publications, he has authored/edited/coedited over 20 books, including *Contemporary Microenterprise, International Social Entrepreneurship, Hispanic Latino Entrepreneurship, Managerial Forensics*, and *Native American Entrepreneurs*. He directs consulting projects worldwide in the areas of strategy formulation, business development, and international finance.

Index

OTHER TITLES IN THE ENTREPRENEURSHIP AND SMALL BUSINESS MANAGEMENT COLLECTION

Scott Shane, Case Western University, *Editor*

- *Startup Strategy Humor: Democratizing Startup Strategy* by Rajesh K. Pillania
- *The Leadership Development Journey: How Entrepreneurs Develop Leadership Through Their Lifetime* by Jen Vuhuong
- *Getting to Market With Your MVP: How to Achieve Small Business and Entrepreneur Success* by J.C. Baker
- *Can You Run Your Business With Blood, Sweat, and Tears? Volume I: Blood* by Stephen Elkins-Jarrett and Nick Skinner
- *Can You Run Your Business With Blood, Sweat, and Tears? Volume II: Sweat* by Stephen Elkins-Jarrett and Nick Skinner
- *Can You Run Your Business With Blood, Sweat, and Tears? Volume III: Tear* by Stephen Elkins-Jarrett and Nick Skinner
- *Family Business Governance: Increasing Business Effectiveness and Professionalism* by Keanon J. Alderson
- *Department of Startup: Why Every Fortune 500 Should Have One* by Ivan Yong Wei Kit and Sam Lee
- *The Rainmaker: Start-Up to Conglomerate* by Jacques Magliolo
- *Get on Board: Earning Your Ticket to a Corporate Board Seat* by Olga V. Mack
- *From Vision to Decision: A Self-Coaching Guide to Starting a New Business* by Dana K. Dwyer
- *Cultivating an Entrepreneurial Mindset* by Tamiko L. Cuellar
- *On All Cylinders, Second Edition: Succeeding as an Entrepreneur and a Leader* by Ron Robinson
- *The Entrepreneurial Adventure: Embracing Risk, Change, and Uncertainty* by David James and Oliver James

Announcing the Business Expert Press Digital Library

Concise e-books business students need for classroom and research

This book can also be purchased in an e-book collection by your library as

- a one-time purchase,
- that is owned forever,
- allows for simultaneous readers,
- has no restrictions on printing, and
- can be downloaded as PDFs from within the library community.

Our digital library collections are a great solution to beat the rising cost of textbooks. E-books can be loaded into their course management systems or onto students' e-book readers.

The **Business Expert Press** digital libraries are very affordable, with no obligation to buy in future years. For more information, please visit **www.businessexpertpress.com/librarians**. To set up a trial in the United States, please email **sales@businessexpertpress.com**.

www.ingramcontent.com/pod-product-compliance
Lightning Source LLC
Chambersburg PA
CBHW061326220326
41599CB00026B/5055